h Beach Lifeguard Stations

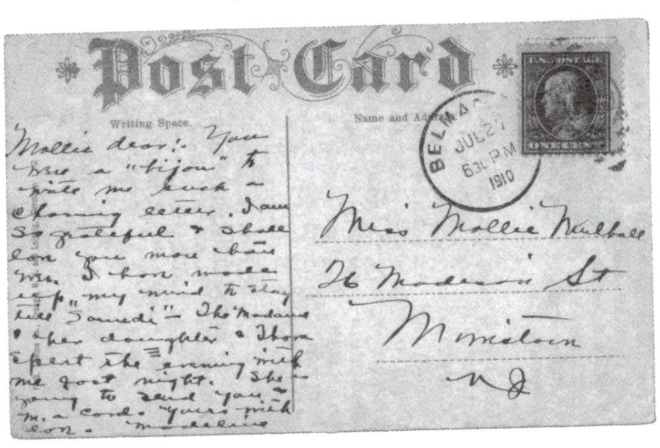

Ready to Write a Book?

Do you collect images of your town or county? Are you passionate about local history, and eager to share what you've learned? If you or your organization always dreamed of writing a book, we would love to hear from you. We are eagerly seeking authors to write illustrated, regional history and guide books. We'd love to hear more about the images you have access to, and the audience you are writing for.

Email your book idea to info@schifferbooks.com, write to Acquisitions, Schiffer Publishing, Ltd. 4880 Lower Valley Rd., Atglen, PA 19310 USA, or call 610-593-1777 to make an appointment to speak with an editor.

South Beach Lifeguard Stations

The Fabulous Life and Lifeguard Stands on Miami Beach's Atlantic Seashore

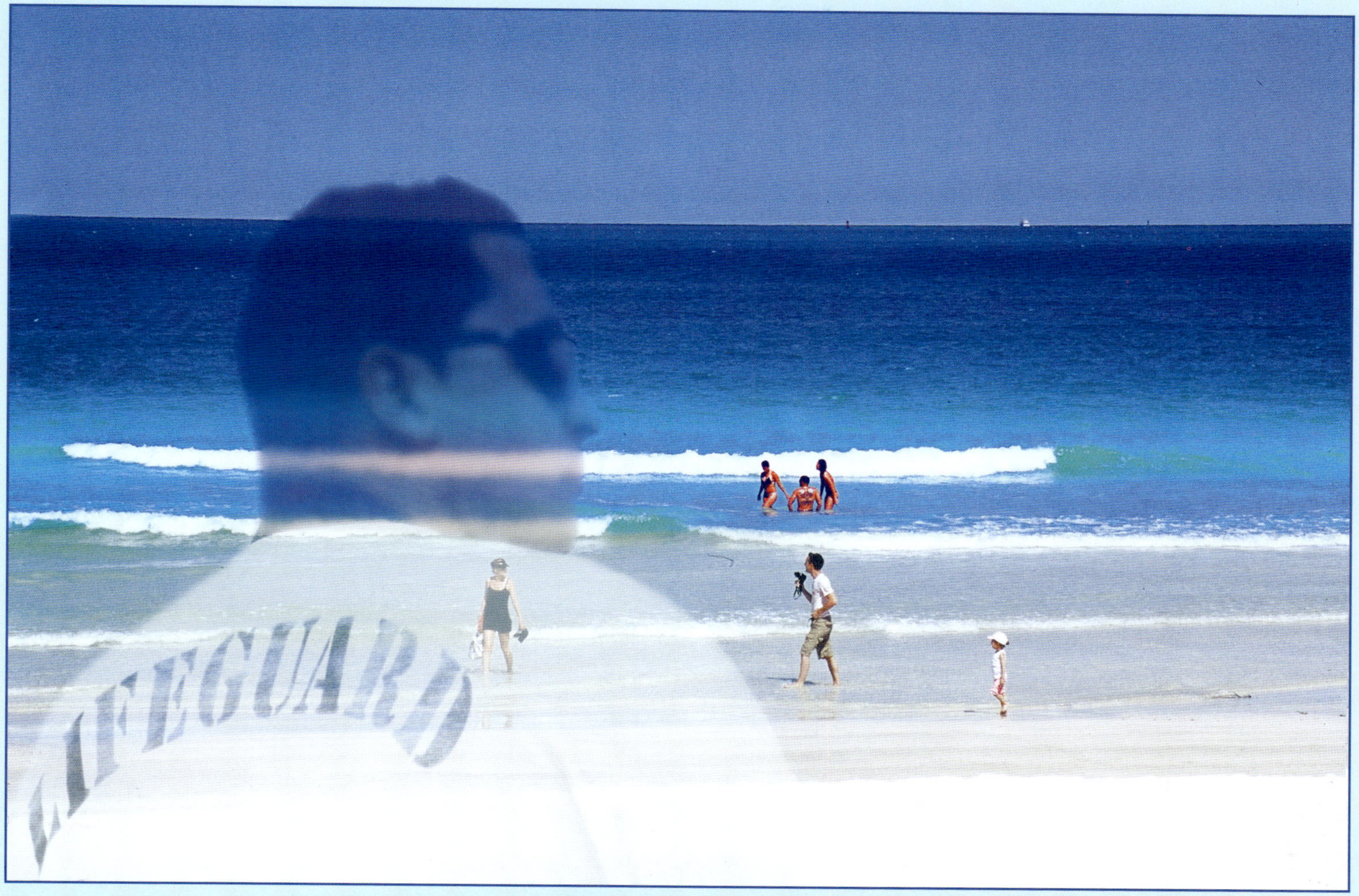

Susan Russell

Schiffer Publishing Ltd

4880 Lower Valley Road Atglen, Pennsylvania 19310

Copyright © 2008 by Susan Russell
Library of Congress Control Number: 2007937652

All rights reserved. No part of this work may be reproduced or used in any form or by any means—graphic, electronic, or mechanical, including photocopying or information storage and retrieval systems—without written permission from the publisher.

The scanning, uploading and distribution of this book or any part thereof via the Internet or via any other means without the permission of the publisher is illegal and punishable by law. Please purchase only authorized editions and do not participate in or encourage the electronic piracy of copyrighted materials.

"Schiffer," "Schiffer Publishing Ltd. & Design," and the "Design of pen and ink well" are registered trademarks of Schiffer Publishing Ltd.

Cover design by Bruce Waters
Type set in Exotc350 DmBd BT/News Gothic BT

ISBN: 978-0-7643-2900-5
Printed in China

Schiffer Books are available at special discounts for bulk purchases for sales promotions or premiums. Special editions, including personalized covers, corporate imprints, and excerpts can be created in large quantities for special needs. For more information contact the publisher.

Published by Schiffer Publishing Ltd.
4880 Lower Valley Road
Atglen, PA 19310
Phone: (610) 593-1777; Fax: (610) 593-2002
E-mail: Info@schifferbooks.com

For the largest selection of fine reference books on this and related subjects, please visit our web site at **www.schifferbooks.com**
We are always looking for people to write books on new and related subjects. If you have an idea for a book please contact us at the above address.

This book may be purchased from the publisher.
Include $3.95 for shipping.
Please try your bookstore first.
You may write for a free catalog.

In Europe, Schiffer books are distributed by
Bushwood Books
6 Marksbury Ave.
Kew Gardens
Surrey TW9 4JF England
Phone: 44 (0) 20 8392-8585;
Fax: 44 (0) 20 8392-9876
E-mail: info@bushwoodbooks.co.uk
Website: www.bushwoodbooks.co.uk
Free postage in the U.K., Europe; air mail at cost.

Dedication

This book is dedicated to my sister, Jane Bauernfeind, a competitive swimmer who became the first female lifeguard on one of South Florida's many famous beaches. Because she loved the sea so much, she spent nearly her entire working life on oceangoing vessels all over the world as a merchant seaman, becoming the first female purser and first chief steward on several shipping lines. During the Desert Storm Persian Gulf War, she was called to duty and flown to Spain to assist in the transport of 2,000-pound bombs on a ship bound for Saudi Arabia, for which she received a civilian commendation.

Acknowledgments

I would like to thank the Miami Beach Property Management Division, including former director Brad A. Judd; Viviana Alemany, Irina Villegas, and Ivo Martinez; Miami Beach Ocean Rescue Division, including Chief Vincent Andreano; Operations Supervisor Henry Oppenborn III, and lifeguards Paul Martinez, Javier Mayor, and Cynthia Aguilar; and, Natalia Fierro and Hilary Russell, all for their invaluable assistance in producing this book.

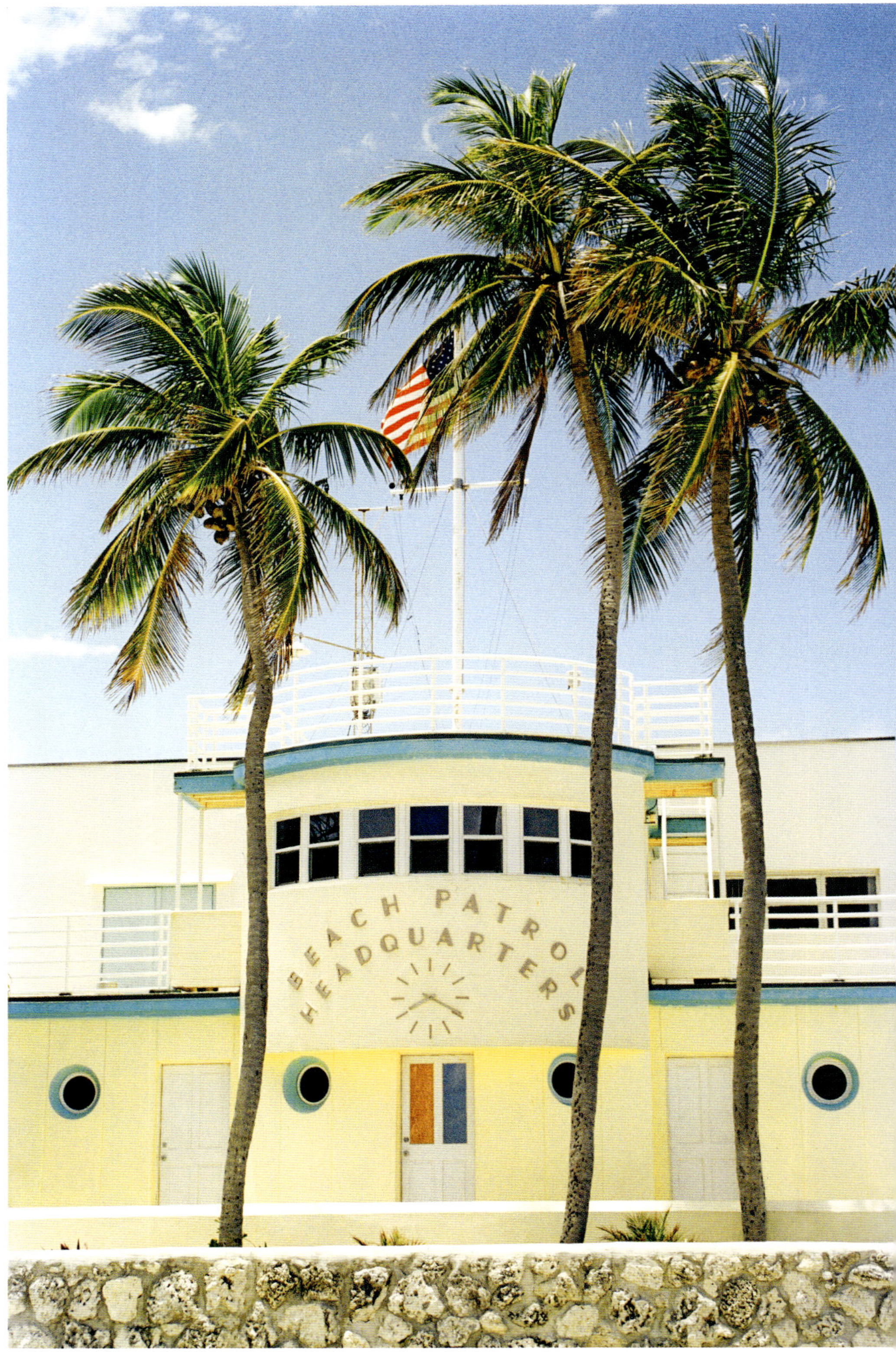

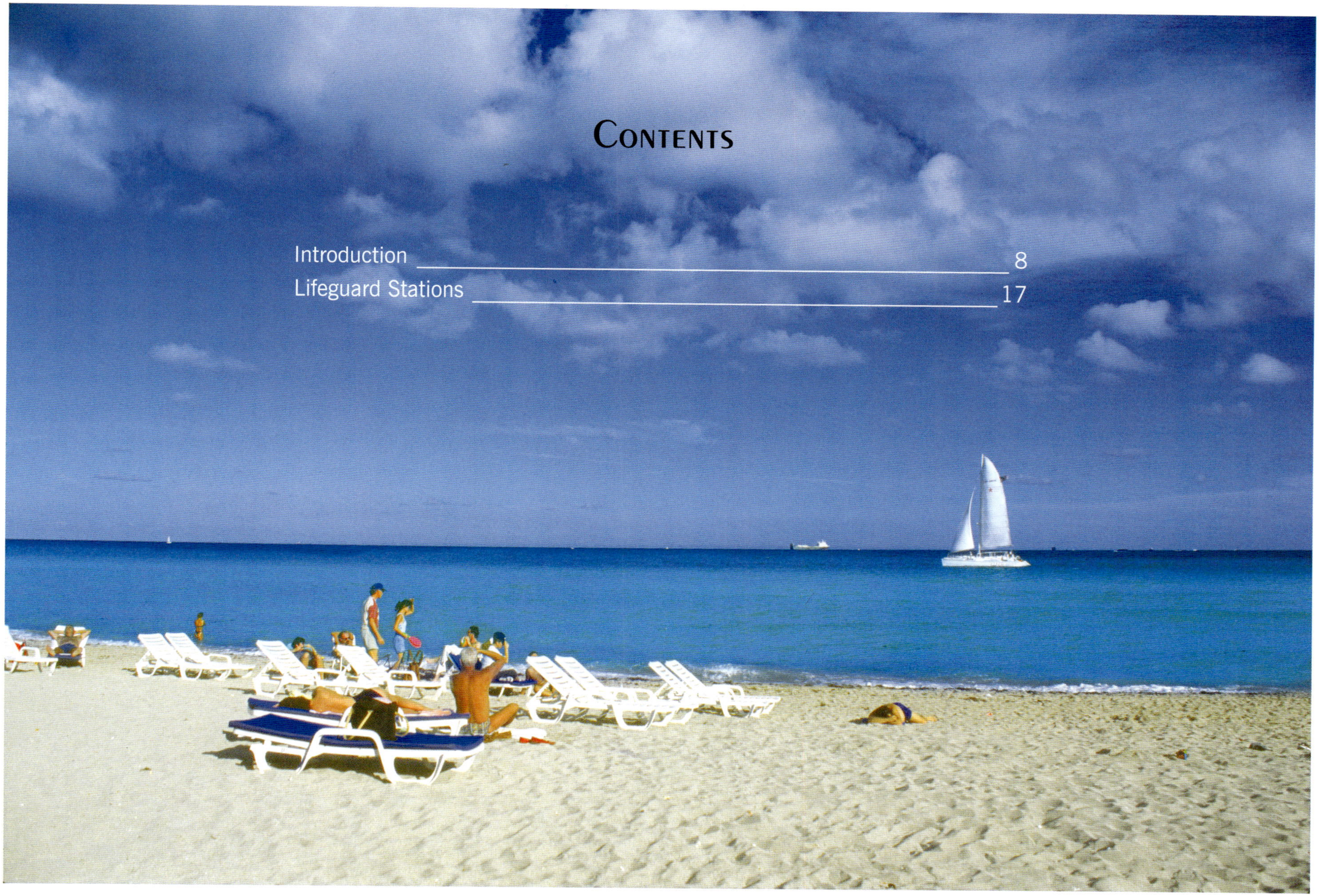

Contents

Introduction

Life on the Atlantic Seashore, along Miami Beach's South Beach and beyond, is a blue sky wonderland of leisure days in aqua waters with billowy white clouds drifting lazily overhead.

Take a moment and run in the surf, twirling salt water as you spin in circles. Float on your back and feel the sea ebb and flow. Dig in the sand till you find a cool, damp space, and then watch as the tide fills it up again. Gaze out on the ocean and see every kind of vessel passing, from sailing ships to fishing boats, from jet skis to yachts, from go-fast boats to cruise ships. Cargo transports hover on the horizon, waiting their turn to come into Government Cut to the loading and unloading docks.

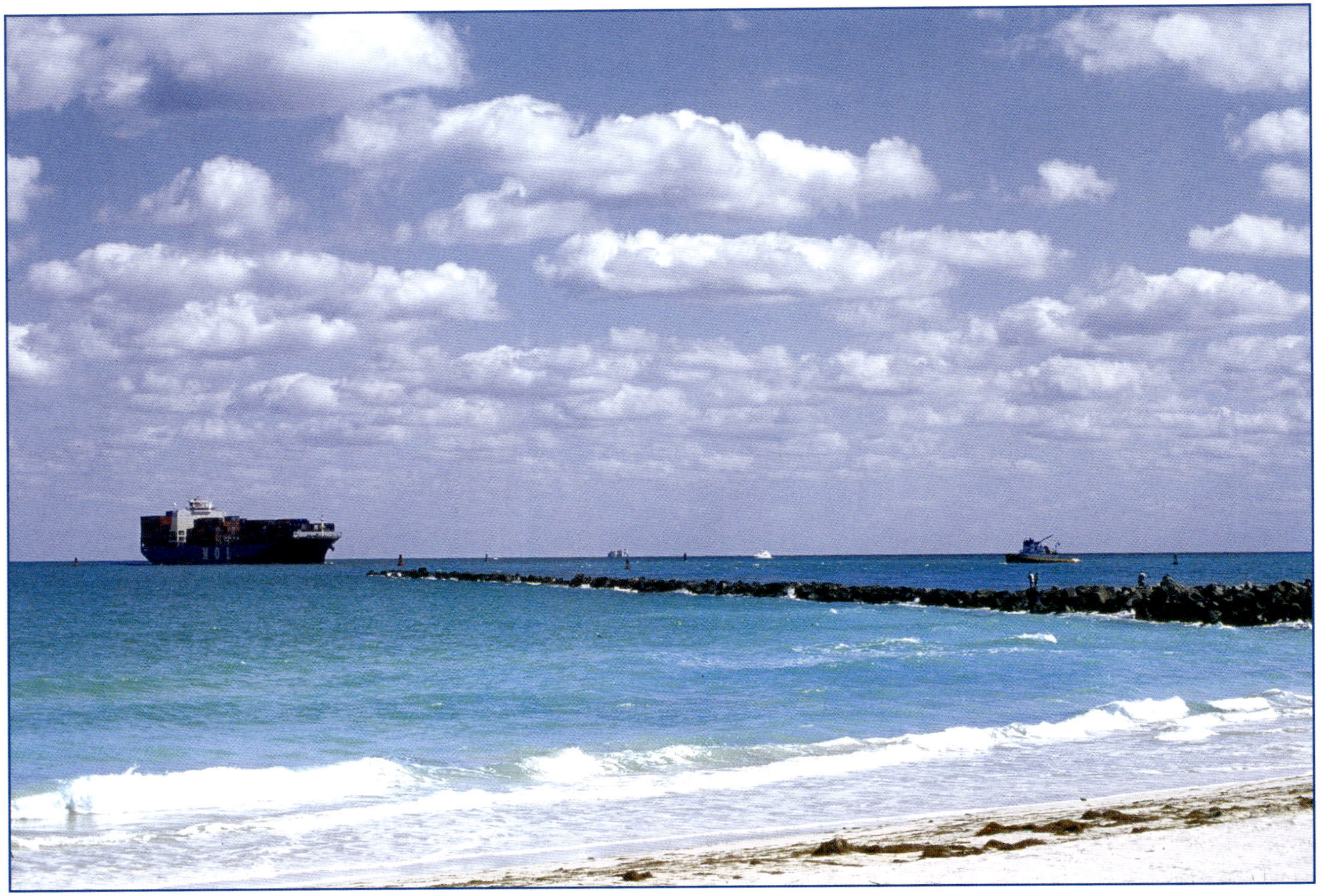

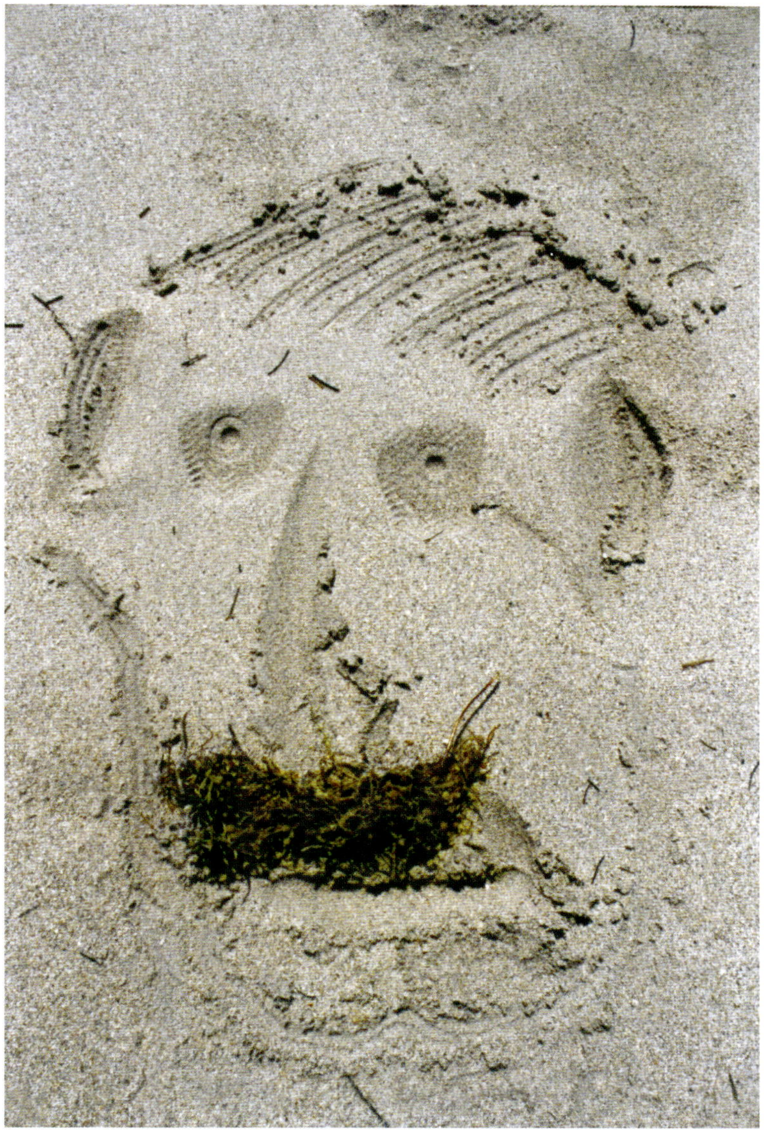

Lounge on the beach on a chaise, a blanket, or under an umbrella or little cabana. Make a sand castle, or etch a funny face with a stick and some seaweed. An actress or model may pass by.

Or, leave the land and go skyward on a parasail to see the magnificent Art Deco vista South Beach is so famous for. Look down for a seagull's view of the sea and the miles-long stretches of beach, where dozens of colorful little buildings stand out on the sand.

These little buildings are the authentic media darlings of South Beach, the whimsical, sometimes wacky, and always charming lifeguard stands that dot the shoreline along SoBe's Atlantic Ocean and points north. Stars of television, movies, and print ads since the 1990s, the colorful and amusing stations are where Miami Beach lifeguards ply their trade, watching over swimmers in the shallows and deeper waters.

Miami Beach has always had lifeguard stands, but it was after Hurricane Andrew in August of 1992 that style trumped sterility. At that point, a whole new concept was brought in to replace the plain, destroyed guardhouses that the powerful Category 5 storm took down.

Noted architect William Lane and renowned artist Kenny Scharf came on board to help design new lifeguard stands that pushed the boundaries of whimsy and defied the description of practical – yet practical they were. Lifeguards were perched higher for better visibility and had more shade from the sometimes stunning sun and heat.

From the outside, these guardhouses resembled tiny houses from a sparkling, crystal world of imagination. There was one with a pretend putting green for a roof. Another had a yellow wave on top. Still another was a big, pink bed. They were gold and purple and shades of green and aqua and lavender. They were the colors of sunshine, afternoon seas, and skies at dawn and dusk ... with a little bubblegum thrown in.

Sandman
A little seaweed and a stick can make a funny face on the beach.

Tourists and residents, both, couldn't believe their eyes at first sight and they rushed to have their pictures taken in front of, alongside of, and up on the lookout decks of these funnier-than-a-comic-book working lifeguard stations.

Word got around and soon the stands were on numerous TV ads, in every travel magazine, and even in the movies as South Beach turned into a popular location site. Models posed, actors acted, ads promoted, and anyone and everyone flocked to the guardhouses for a look-see and a keep-sake picture.

In addition to the famous architect and artist, others also got on board in designing guardhouses after Andrew, including the Beach Patrol itself and the School of Architecture at Florida International University.

Everything was going along fine until the fall of 2005, when once again South Florida took hits from hurricanes, and some of the iconic guardhouses went down in those storms.

But, amidst the damage, all was not lost, either in the several unique guardhouses that survived, or in the imaginations at work to replace the ones that didn't.

This time the City of Miami Beach set out to build the lifeguard stands stronger and make them movable, if needed. They also built them still higher for an even better panorama for the lifeguards. And they built them with varied palettes of color and a kind of bas-relief decorations.

One new guard station soars skyward as a lighthouse, complete with glassed in tower and dramatic painted horizontal stripes in bright red and white. Another stand is decorated in painted faux surfboards with tropical flowers in a dozen hues tacked onto the deep aqua structure. Still another sports a cutout version of the Miami Beach logo of a sail, the sun, and waves, in deep blue, yellow, and white.

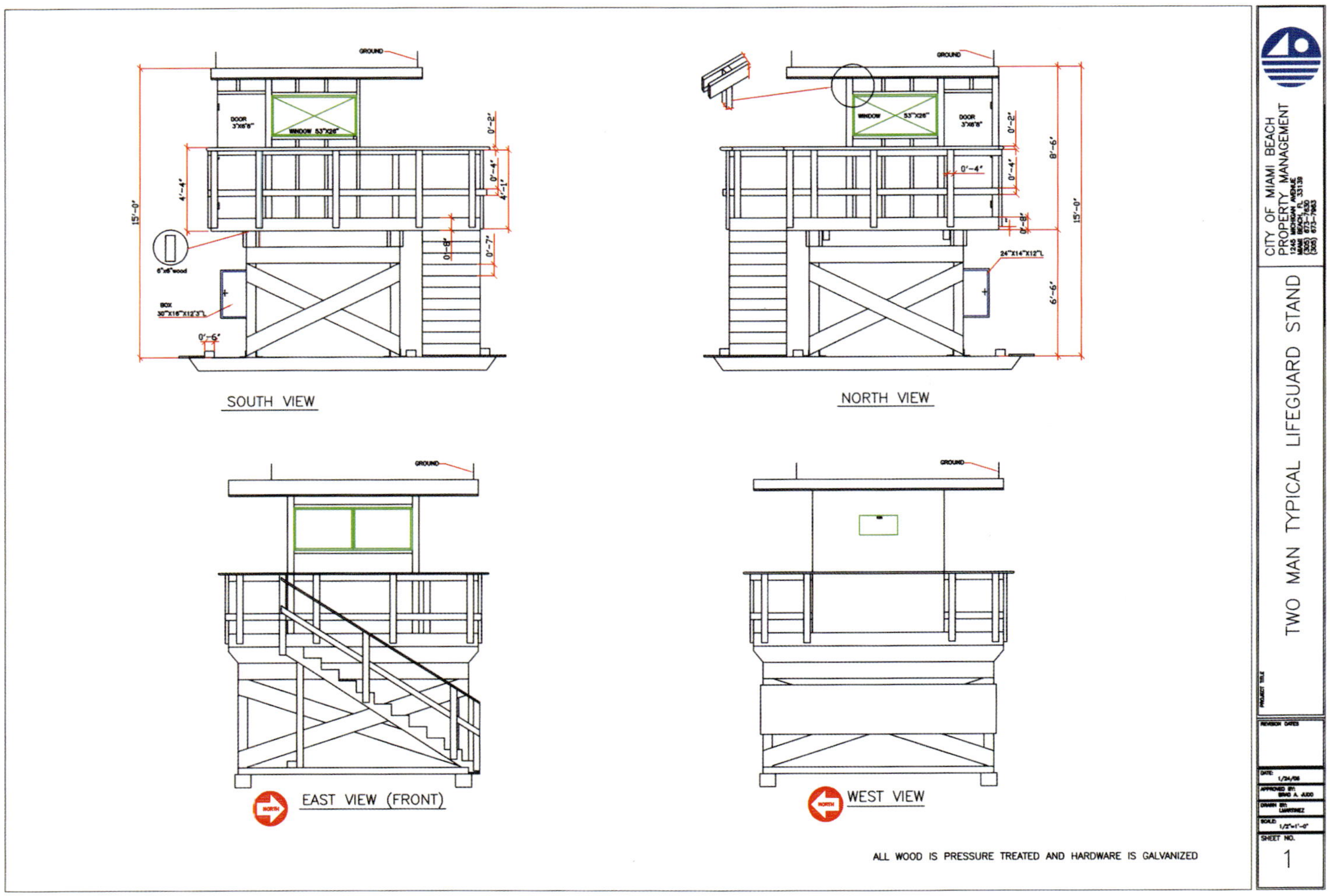

Architectural Plan for a Guardhouse
A typical lifeguard stand could be built as a teahouse or a playhouse. *Drawing courtesy of the Miami Beach Property Management Division.*

There's one covered in colorful ceramic sealife figurines made by Miami Beach schoolchildren, another has the look of the American Flag. And still another wears a golden sun on a deep lavender backdrop, with yellow-green shamrocks attached on all four sides. These are some of the new guardhouses.

Of the icons, the most famous still stands as it has since the mid-1990s. Colored deep bubblegum pink, it's a totally round ship's turret, or perhaps a spaceship (your choice!), complete with a swirling, Wizard of Oz-like antenna topped by a pink ball, said to be able to guide one to or from any magical dream place.

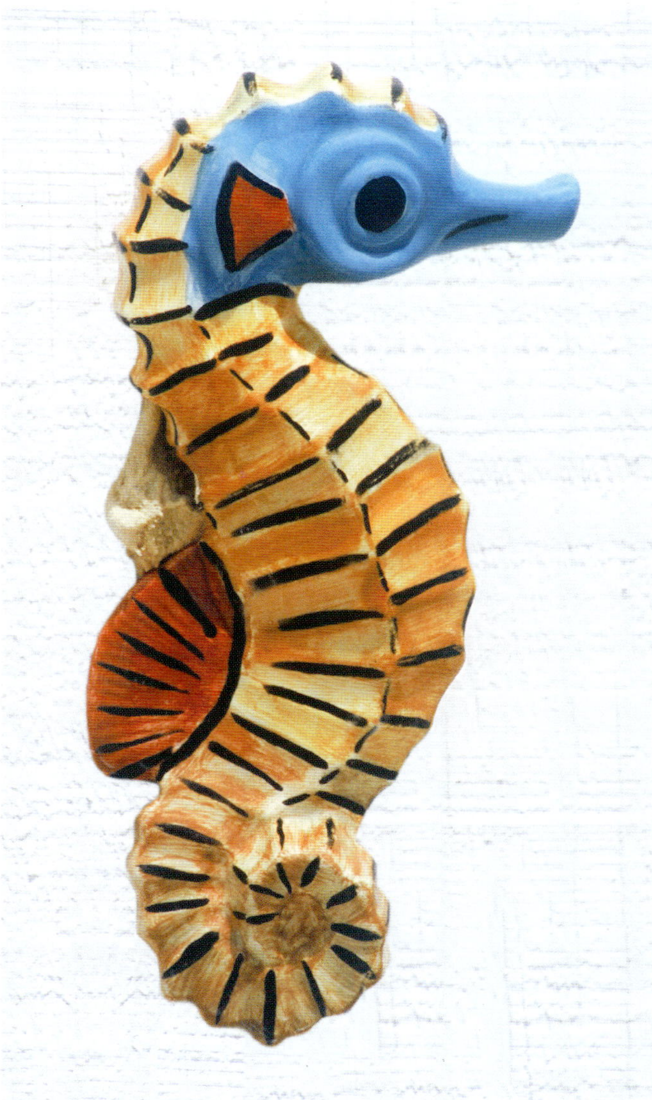

Seahorse
Little decorative seahorse adorns the 17ST guardhouse.

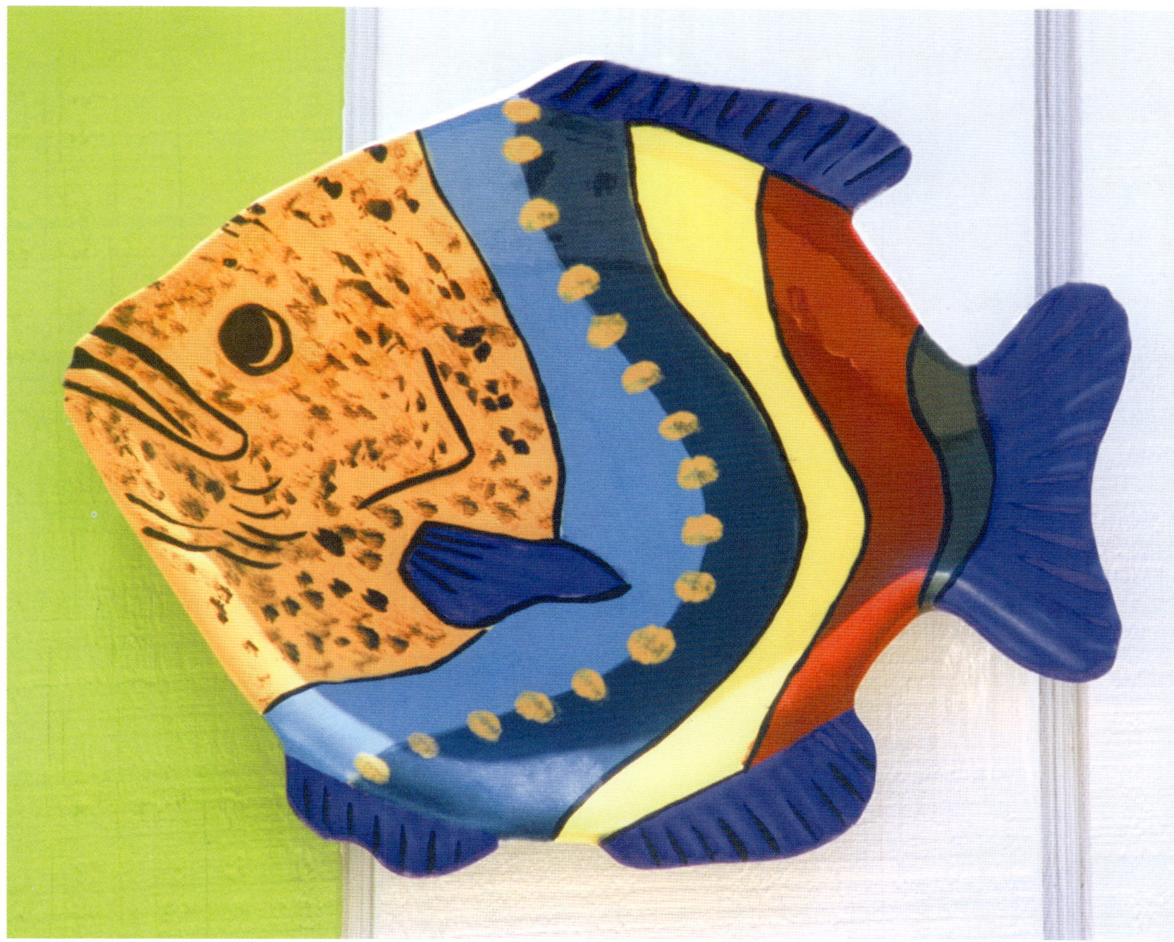

Fish
Colorful ceramic fish adorns the same guardhouse.

Today, that station and the others, new and old, make a total of twenty-nine working lifeguard stations on Miami Beach, starting at South Pointe next to the jetty and going all the way up to 85th Street. Some 100+ professional lifeguards man these stations seven days a week, for nine hours a day for nine months, and seven hours a day in the three winter months. They are highly trained and dedicated men and women who are called upon to use their strength, ingenuity, goodwill, and diplomacy, at any given moment and in any given situation, to save a life, reassure a frightened swimmer, calm a rowdy group, or answer a question from a curious tourist. They are called upon to be heroes on a regular basis, and they answer the call without a moment's hesitation.

Of their numbers, some ten percent are women. One of those women recently completed a fifty-eight-mile, non-stop journey from Cat Cay in the Bahamas to South Florida on a twelve-foot paddleboard using only her hands, breaking a world's record in the process. One of her male counterparts recently won a paddleboard race circling twelve miles around Key West, besting more than thirty competitors. Many other guards, of course, have achieved notable honors throughout the years since the 1926 inception of the lifesaving unit on Miami Beach.

The lifeguards and their directors – the chief and the operations supervisor – are collectively called the Miami Beach Ocean Rescue Division and with their two office staff are an official part of the Miami Beach Fire Department. Some of the lifeguards go on to join the regular fire department.

These very fit lifeguards are not the only ones on the beach who can and do work out to keep healthy and strong, and if a beachgoer were so inclined, a walk (a long, long walk) could be made on various kinds of pathways from the jetty all the way to the last guardhouse on 85th Street. At the jetty, there is a short boardwalk that turns into a pink, brick walkway that will eventually be extended in some form all the way to the start of Lummus Park on 5th Street and Ocean Drive.

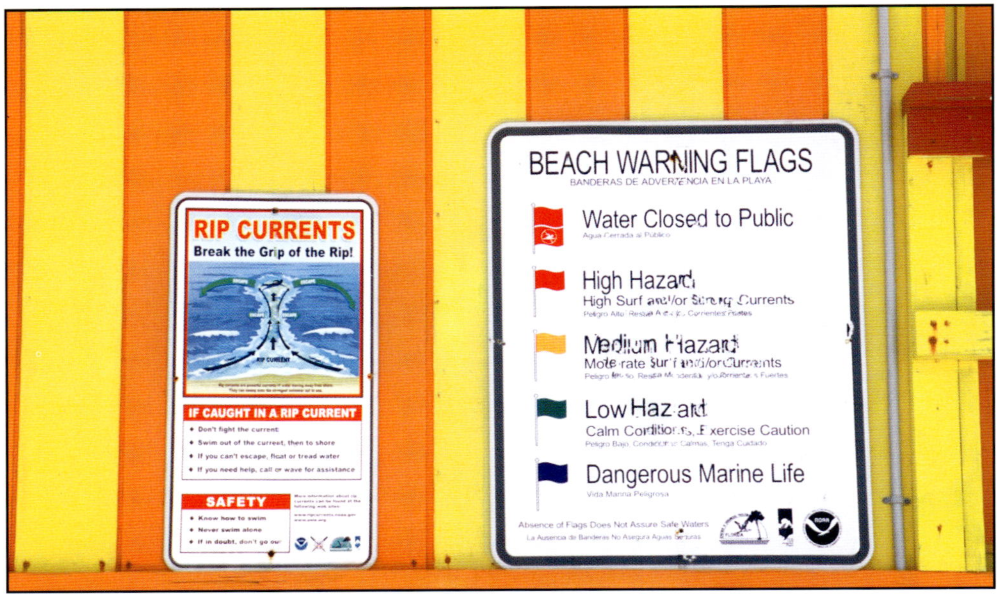

Beach Conditions Alert

Every lifeguard stand displays signs explaining the significance of various posted flags and instructions on escaping rip currents.

Along the park, from 5th to 14th streets, a wide and sometimes curving sidewalk runs alongside a low and historic coral rock wall that separates the start of the sand and beach from the grassy and palm tree-laden park. There are volleyball nets in the sand just off the sidewalk near 7th Street. And the path along the park is one of the areas where skaters and others on wheels are allowed. Along the way, there are sturdy park chairs painted tropical aqua and outdoor showers to match.

Many of the beach locales offer showers and a variety of seating and resting areas. There are also several public restrooms.

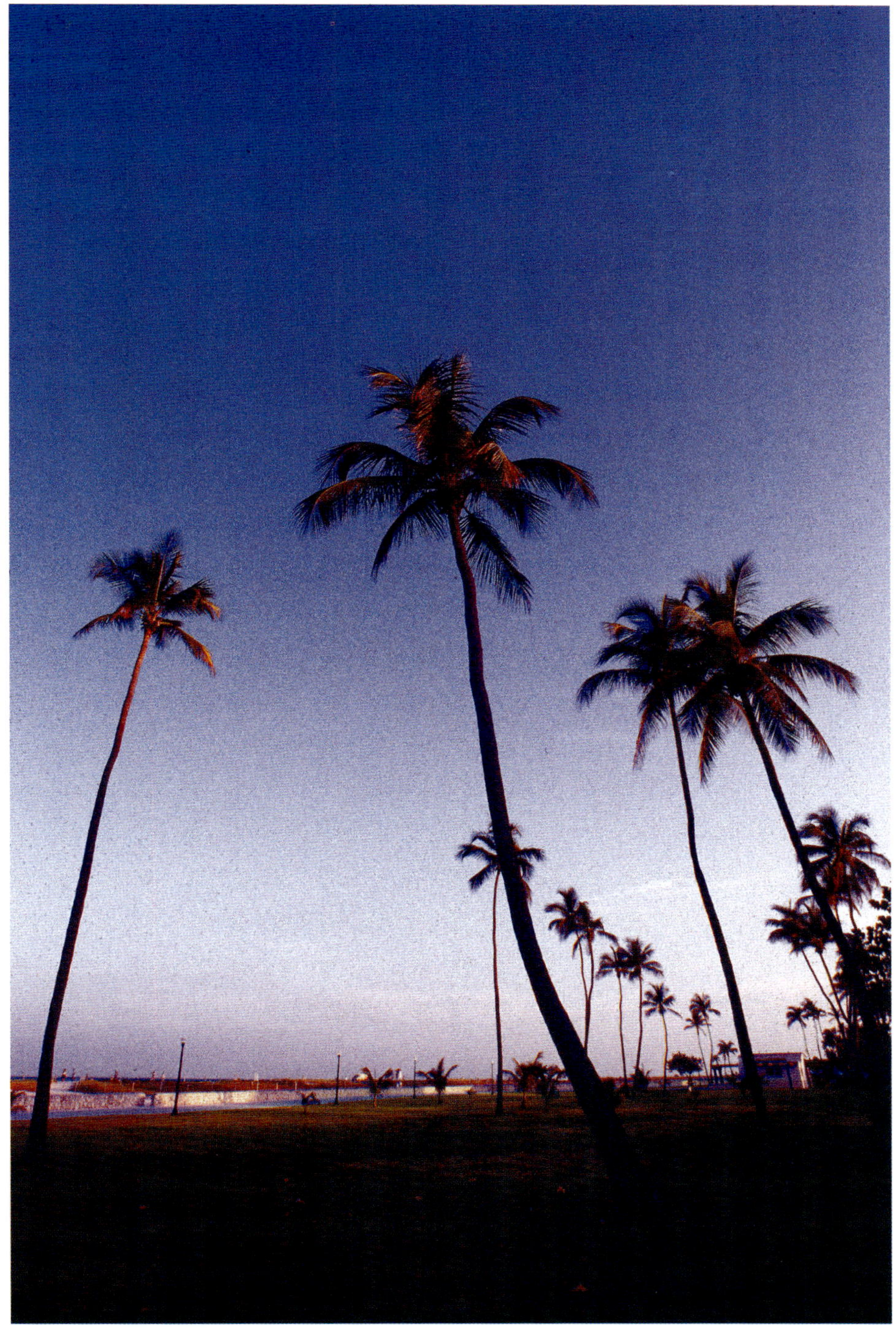

Palms at Dusk
A pink sky eases South Beach into the night amidst a backdrop of magnificent palm trees.

Beginning on 2lst Street, a wonderfully wide, wooden, elevated boardwalk meanders all the way up to 47th Street. Wheels and pets are not allowed, but it is a runner's and walker's paradise as it provides shady shelters with benches along the way and a view of the sea that is breathtaking. Here, you'll also have an opportunity to see the variety of vegetation that grows in the protected sand dunes between the beach and the boardwalk, including the still scarce and highly protected sea oats.

The beach continues to run uninterrupted as it goes into the higher street numbers up to the last guardhouse, where condominiums, small hotels, and older residential and commercial neighborhoods border the beaches.

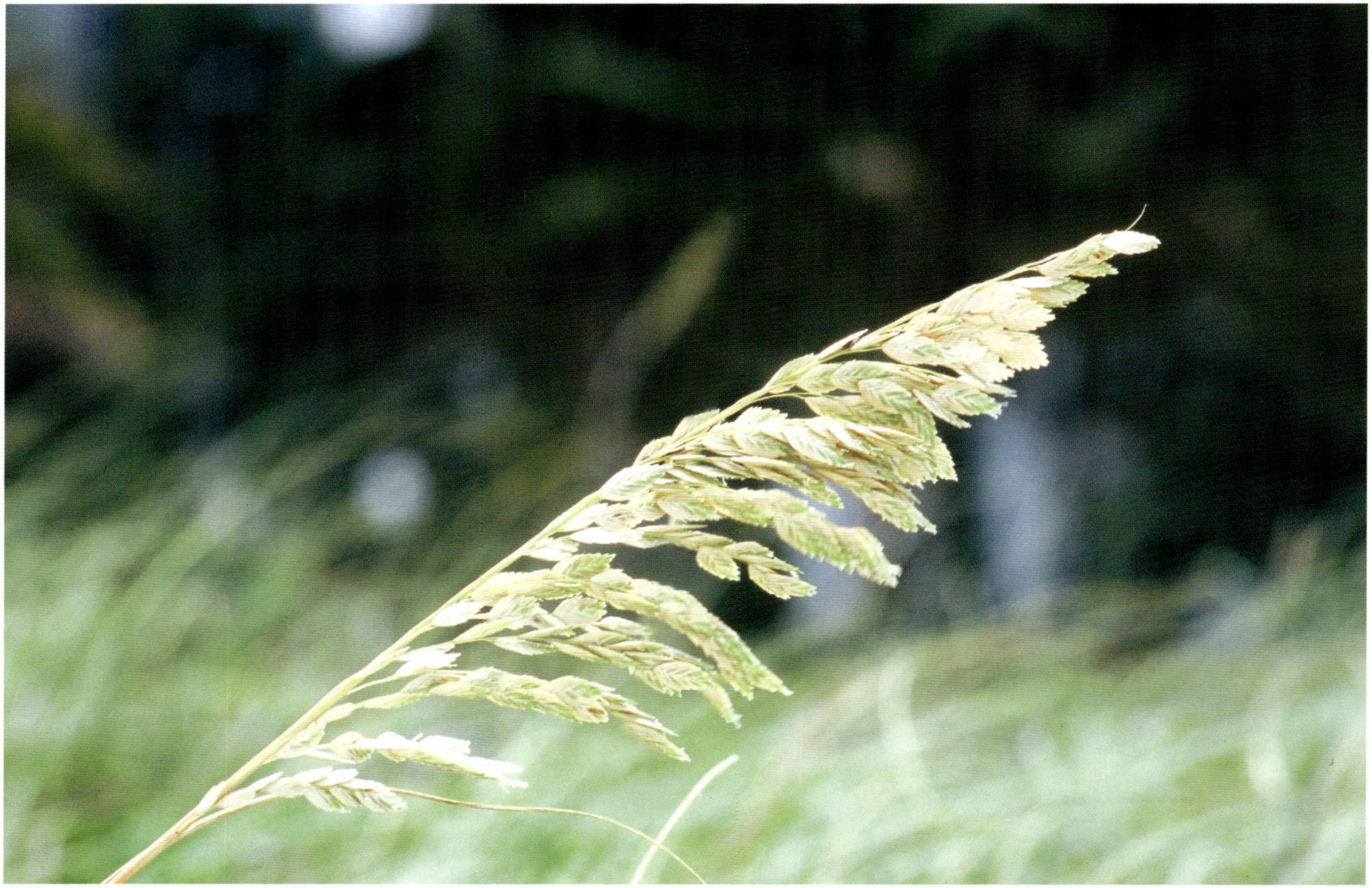

Sea Oat
A delicate sea oat takes root in a Miami Beach sand dune.

Parking, sometimes the caveat to a great day or evening, is easily found on certain days and in less busy locales, and going early is a good recommendation for any of the more popular sites. Bring plenty of quarters and a good watch. Resist choosing a marked area that's clearly a no parking zone. Better to circle for a while and wait for someone to leave, or find one of several parking garages, than to face the consequences after a long day at the beach. Dining at a nearby restaurant as part of your beach day, especially on famous Ocean Drive, might get you valet parking for a reasonable fee, but probably with a time limit.

For sure, the one thing you want to have on the beach is plenty of time to breathe in the sea air, feel the salt spray, and absorb the limitless colors of Miami Beach's Atlantic Ocean and its seashore of amazing lifeguard stands.

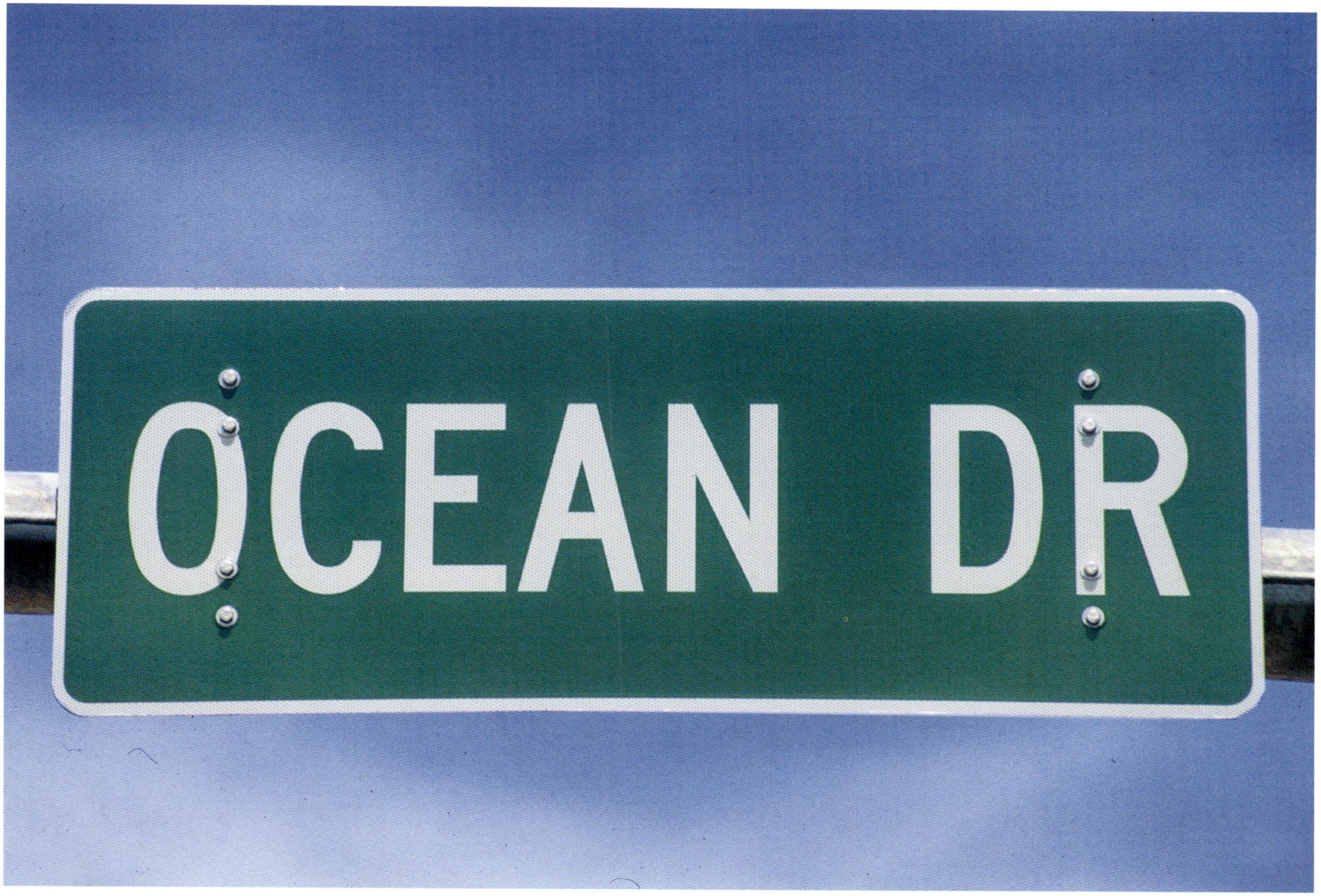

Ocean Drive Sign
Ocean Drive street sign somewhere between First Street in South Pointe and 14th Street on the north end of Lummus Park.

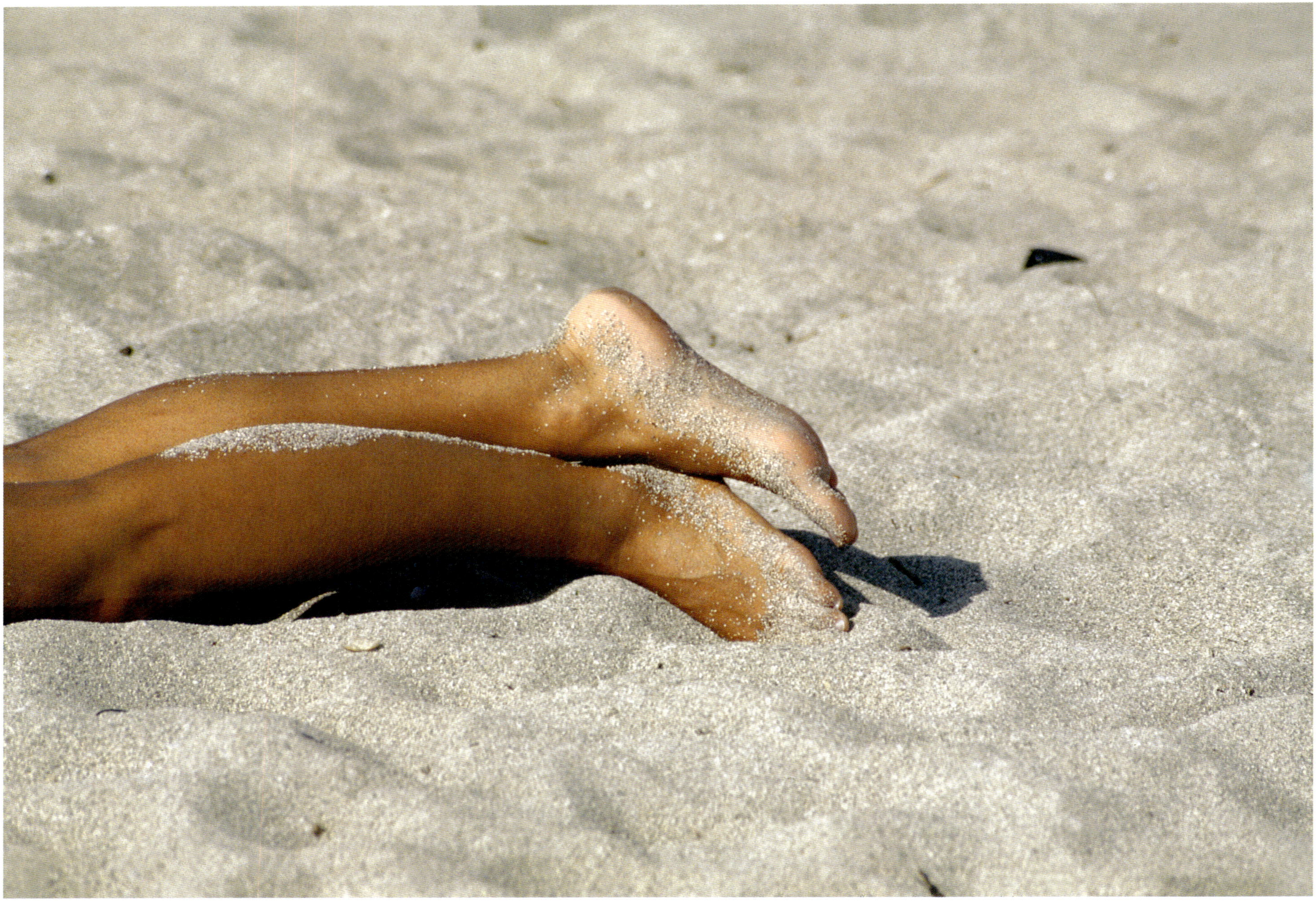

Legs on the Sand
Settling onto the warm sand is like melding into an inviting blanket.

Lifeguard Stations

Jetty Guardhouse

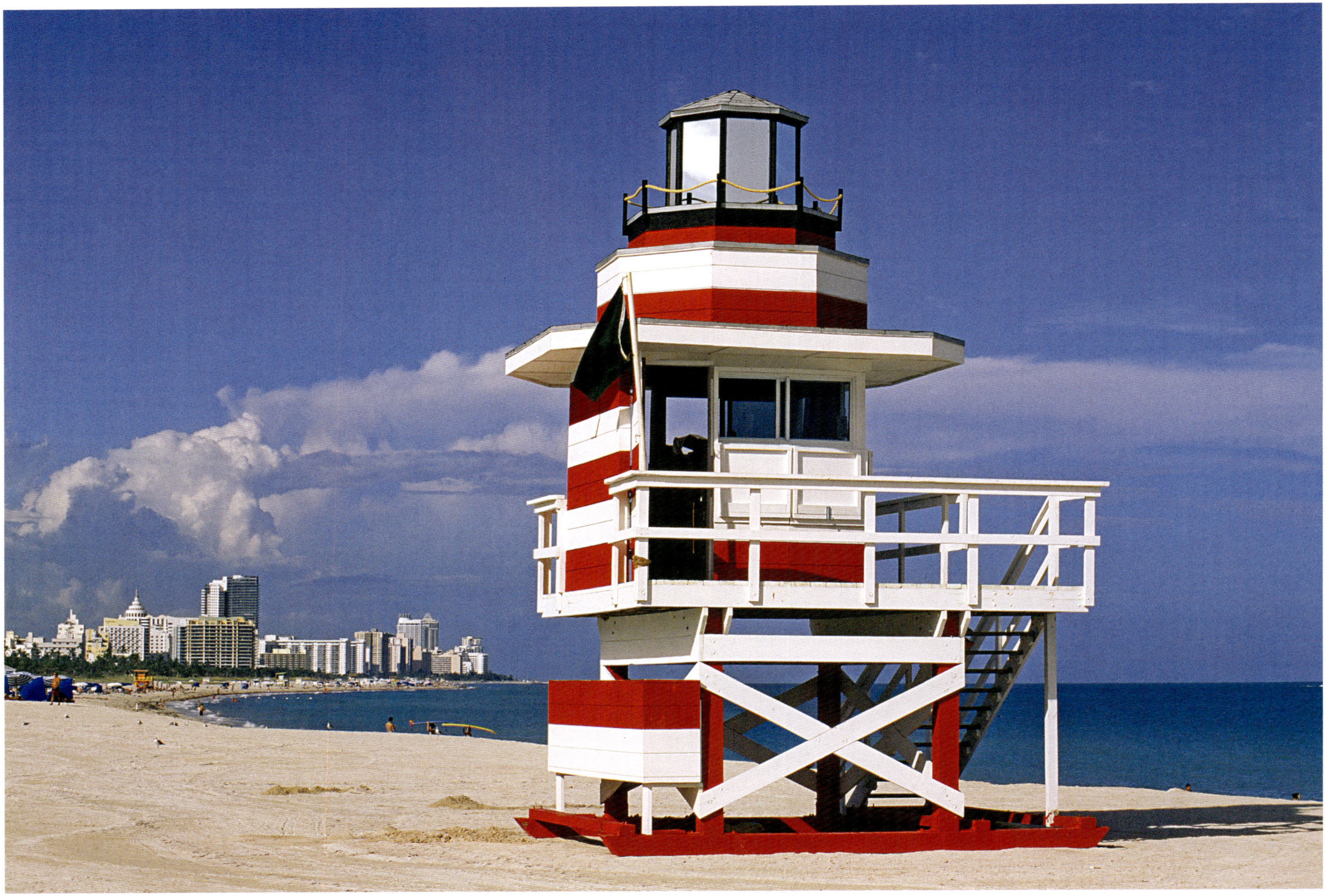

This is South Pointe, an area of elegance and hipness. Your journey into the life and lifeguard stands of Miami Beach's famous Atlantic shoreline begins here at the jetty, the southernmost point of South Beach, as you step onto the glowing November sands and view the architectural delight often called the "Lighthouse Guardhouse." Striped in bright red and white, with its own reflective glass tower, what makes this lighthouse authentic is the lifeguard who mans it, watching over swimmers under usually blue skies and white clouds streaming over turquoise waters with little lapping waves.

The actual jetty, to the right and south of the guardhouse by a few feet, extends out in rugged rocks. This beach section is a great place to see the big and small ships emerge from Government Cut, the deep channel in and out from the commercial docks. Across the cut is Fisher Island, home to the rich and famous, accessible only by ferry.

Turn to the left and see the whole vista of South Beach and beyond present itself as the shoreline curves around and takes the eye miles to the North. Art Deco architecture is everywhere. Wonderful buildings have been preserved, thanks to the Miami Design Preservation League (MDPL) and its foundress, Barbara Capitman, whose visionary determination spearheaded not only the local preservation of Art Deco, but inspired the worldwide movement a short thirty years ago.

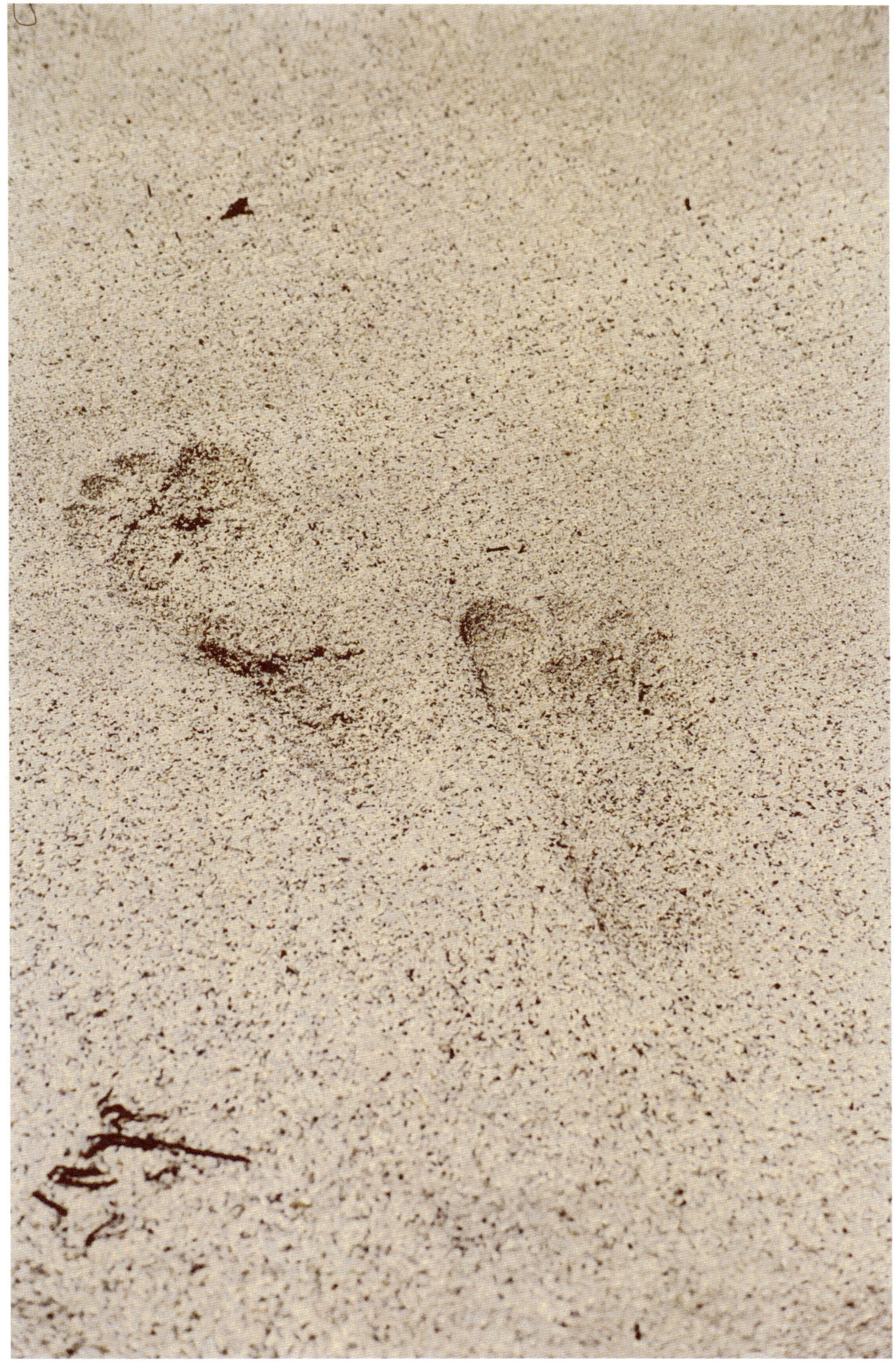

100T-Towers Guardhouse

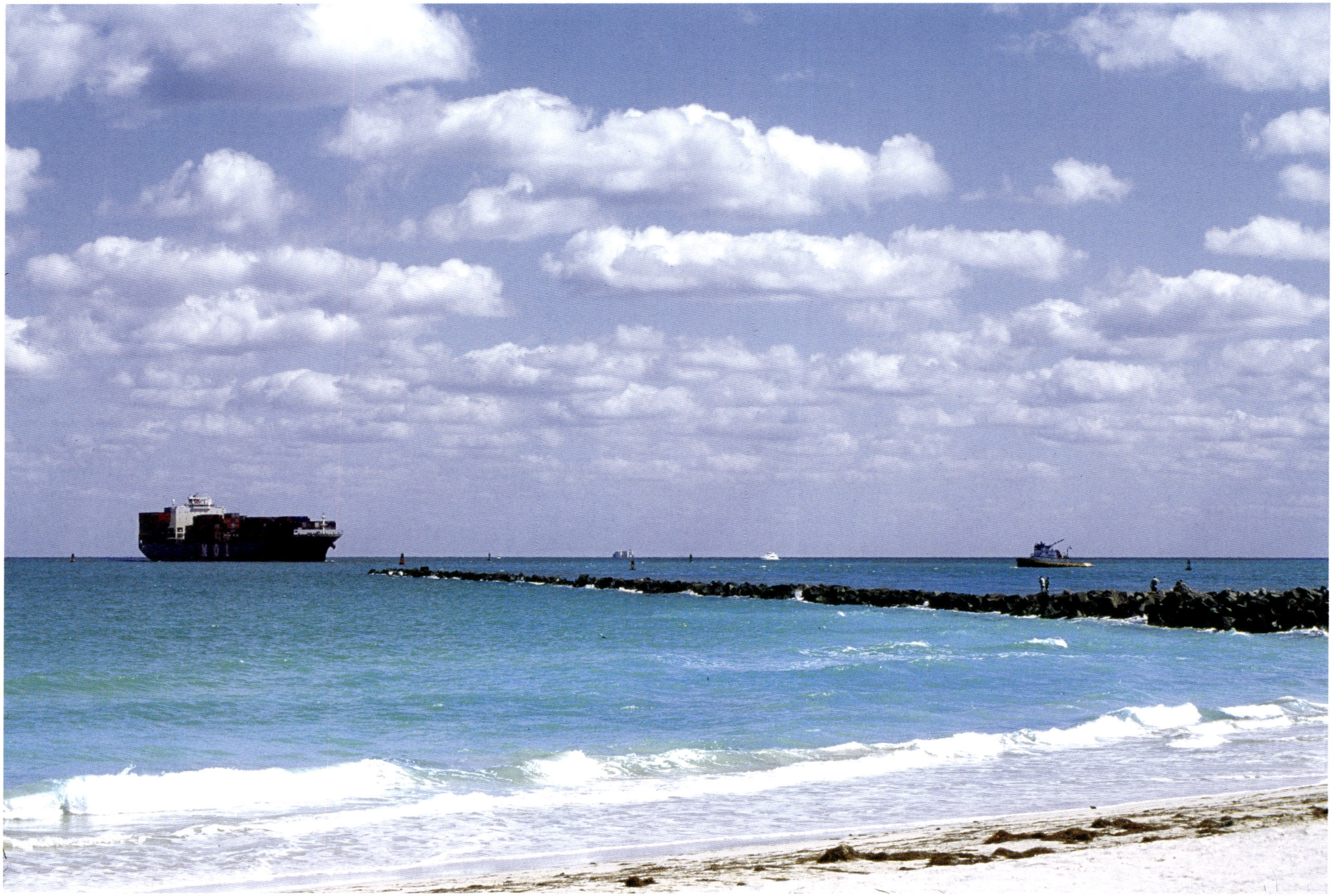

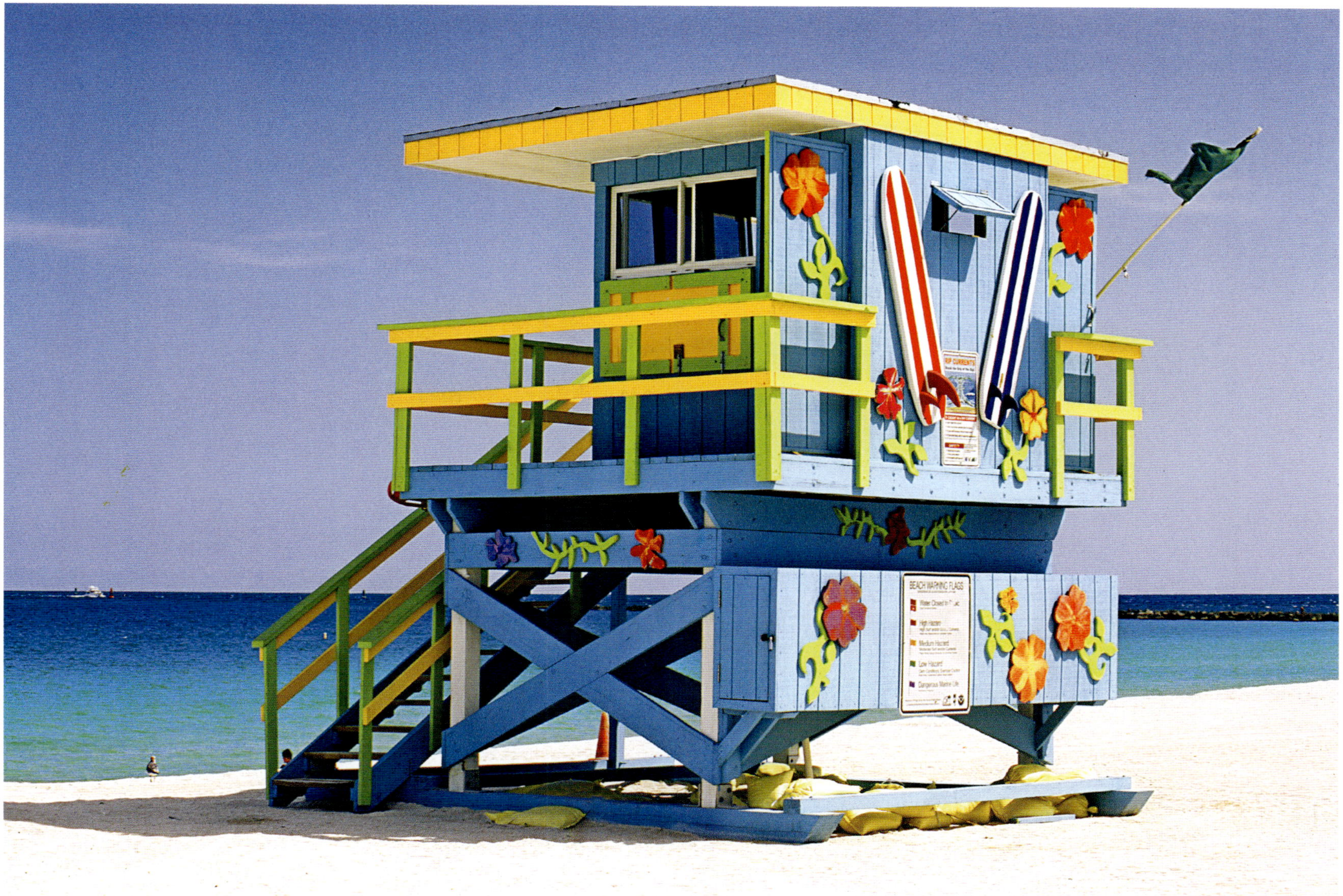

This amazing guardhouse has so much color and splash, it's become one of the favorite places for photographs. It's located a short distance up the beach from The Lighthouse and is officially known as the Towers Guardhouse, or 100T. I call it "The Surfboard." It's within sight of the jetty and it's another choice spot to sit and watch the ships coming in and out. The surf here is usually gentle (watch the warning flags to confirm this), and it's a great place for the kids to play.

This September day, the guardhouse displays a green flag, a signal that the water is calm and no dangerous marine life (such as jelly fish) has been observed. Caution, however, is always the rule of the day when swimming in any open body of water. Consult the lifeguard if you have questions.

Behind the beach here rises a phenomenon seen all over South Florida now, multiple sky-high condominiums appearing in an array of colors and interesting shapes, either completed or in the process of being built. The cranes will tell you which.

There is no direct street access to this guardhouse and the best way to get to it, as well as The Lighthouse, is by way of the next guardhouse north, located on 1st Street in South Pointe.

1ST Guardhouse

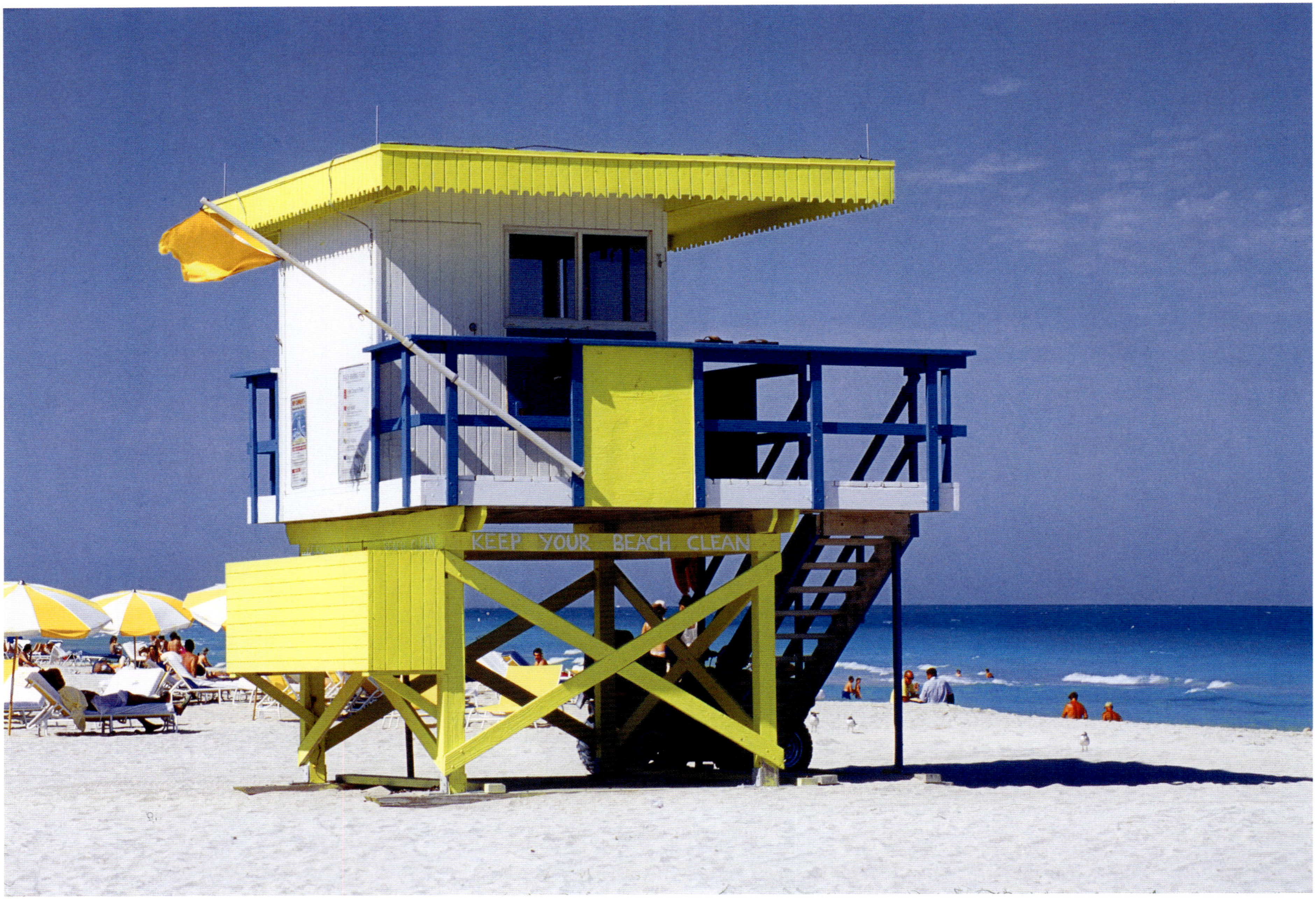

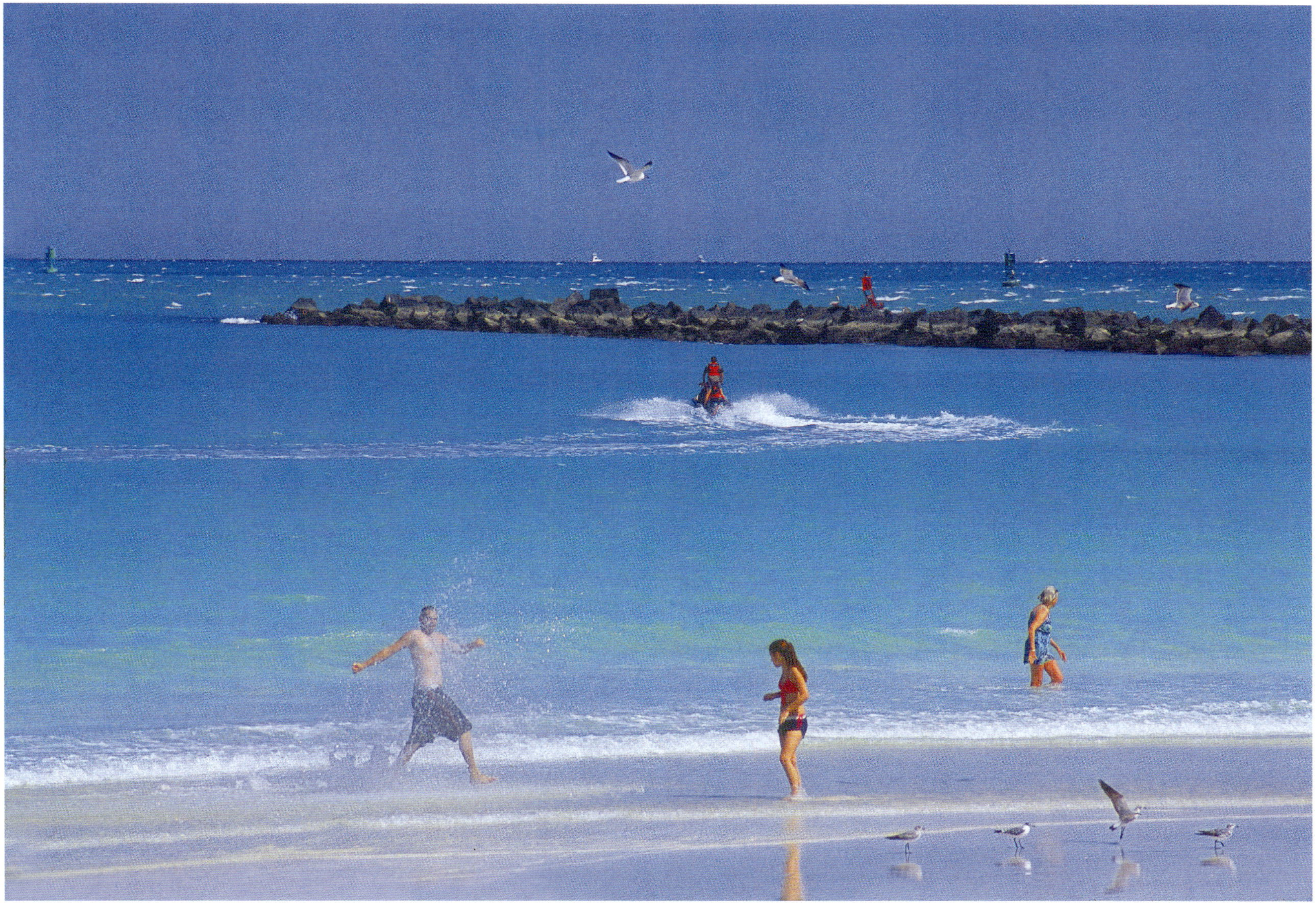

First Street on the beach is the home of this simple, but brilliantly colored lifeguard stand. Officially called the 1ST Guardhouse, (ST meaning street), it could also be called the "Edgy Roof Guardhouse," because it has roof edges that one can only imagine challenged the carpenter to the extreme with its alternate cuts of a half-circle, half-triangle, and half-rectangle all the way around. The sunshine yellow, deep blue, and bright white paint stand out even from a distance, as one approaches from the First Street entrance on South Pointe. The April day this photograph was taken, the sky was idyllic and the sea a perfect turquoise.

Beachgoers splashed and played while a jet-skier headed out toward the jetty. Look out a little further and see a horizon often dotted by cargo ships, yachts, fishing boats, sailing vessels or maybe a cruise ship running past the channel markers.

Glance skyward and there may be the occasional seaplane going by, or small planes pulling advertising banners. And, of course, there are the seagulls, some white, some speckled with grey or brown. They'll arrive by the dozens if someone comes up with a few crumbs for them to eat. However, not all sunbathers are delighted to see the gulls show up.

It's worth knowing that just steps from the 1ST Guardhouse are restaurants, clubs, a market, a bank, a cafe, and an ATM.

Old 3ST Guardhouse – Dawn and Dusk

This little after-Andrew guardhouse wasn't awake yet on a beautiful November morning, as the moon still hung in the pink sky waiting to see if any beachgoers were going to show up. They would have had the tranquil scene all to themselves. A place for dreaming, sipping coffee, and early morning relaxation, it was still quite a few hours before the coming intensity of the semi-tropical sun.

The guardhouse is gone, but the mood never is – for those brave enough to be on the beach at 6 a.m.

Dusk is another magical time on the beach, where the colors of dawn are often duplicated. This July evening, just before 6 p.m., heavy rains had ceased and the white cruise ship with the whale's tail came sliding by on Government Cut heading into a giant, pink cloud mural. Just as the liner passed, its sister ship – which had gone out to sea in a rainstorm half-an-hour earlier – presented itself on the horizon like an illusion.

Monday and Friday evenings from 5 p.m. on are good times to watch the cruise ships from anywhere near the jetty.

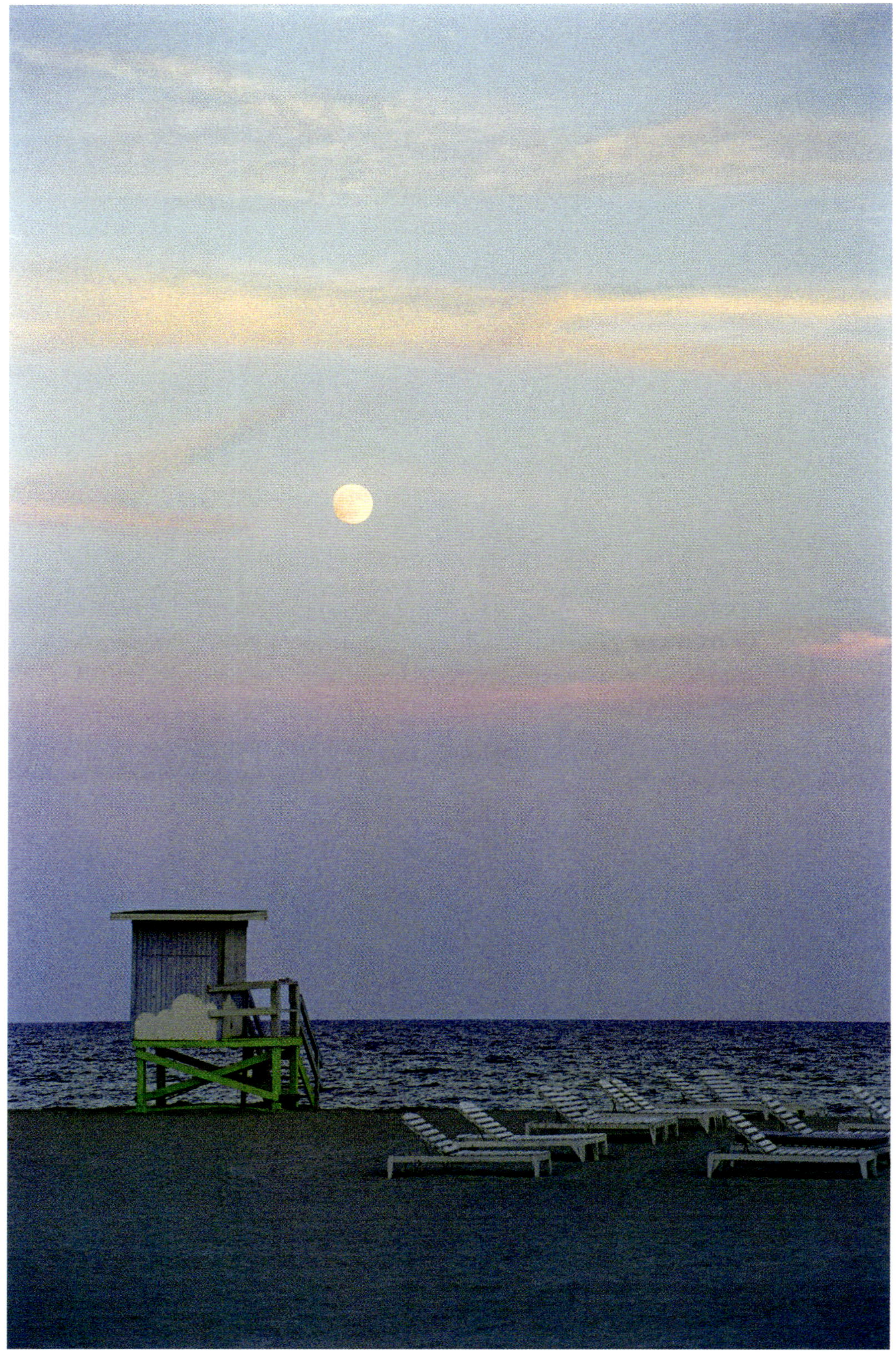

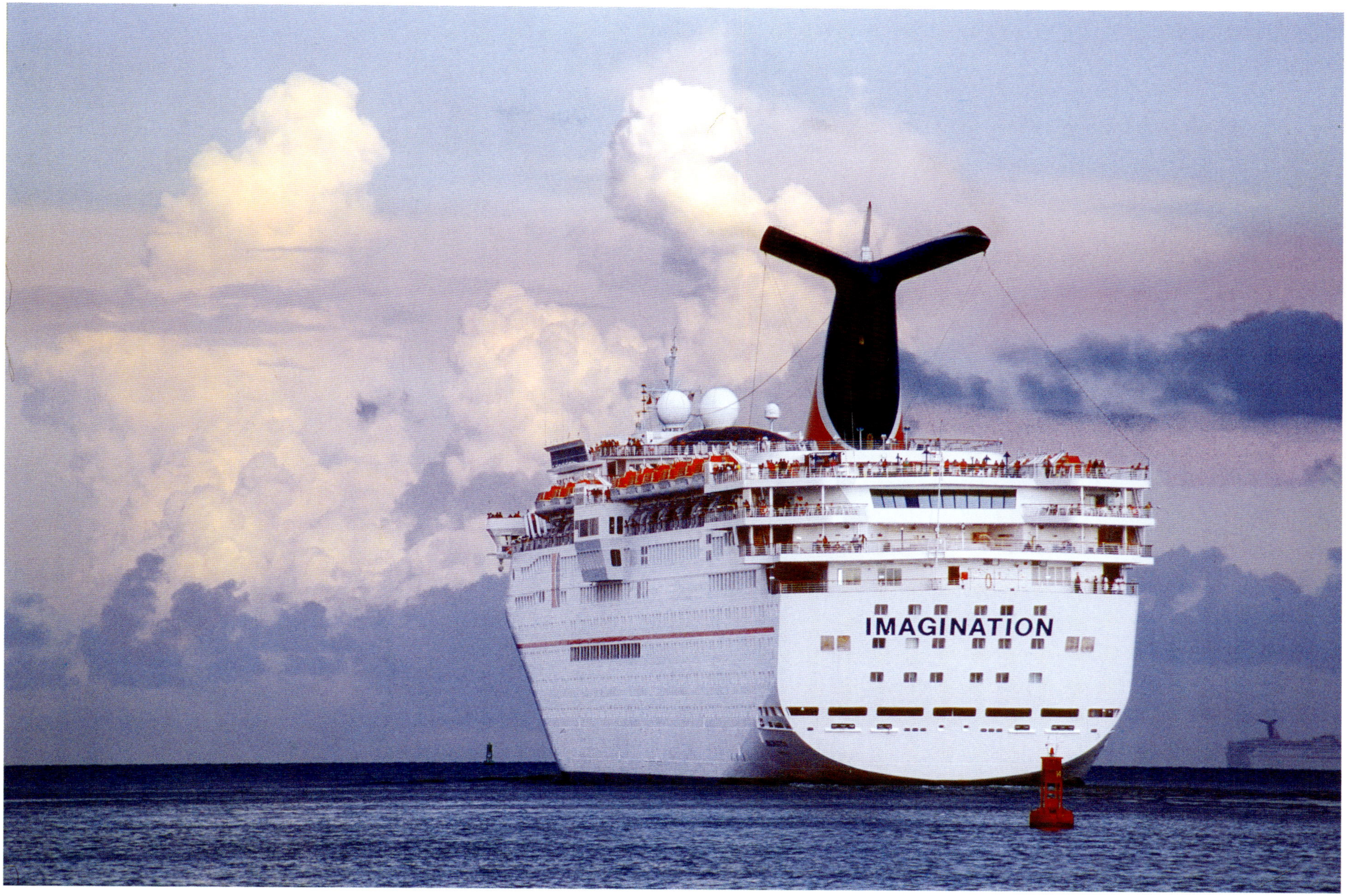
IMAGINATION

3ST Guardhouse

Yellow and orange vertical stripes announce the 3ST Guardhouse, and it would be hard to miss this lifeguard station anywhere on the beach. In fact, this guardhouse has moved around a bit, but now seems to have found a permanent home on the Third Street site.

It was an exquisitely calm and quiet day that set the scene for this September photograph, with the seas flat, flat, flat. The beach was not crowded, as expected just as summer concludes and the school year starts up.

The first hint of chill in the air in the Northeast of the country will, however, send the snowbirds flocking to South Beach once again.

Meanwhile, South Florida residents will fill up the beaches without competition, especially on weekends.

An impressive yacht and a seemingly tiny helicopter complete the scene on a different, not quite so flat seas, but still perfect, South Beach day.

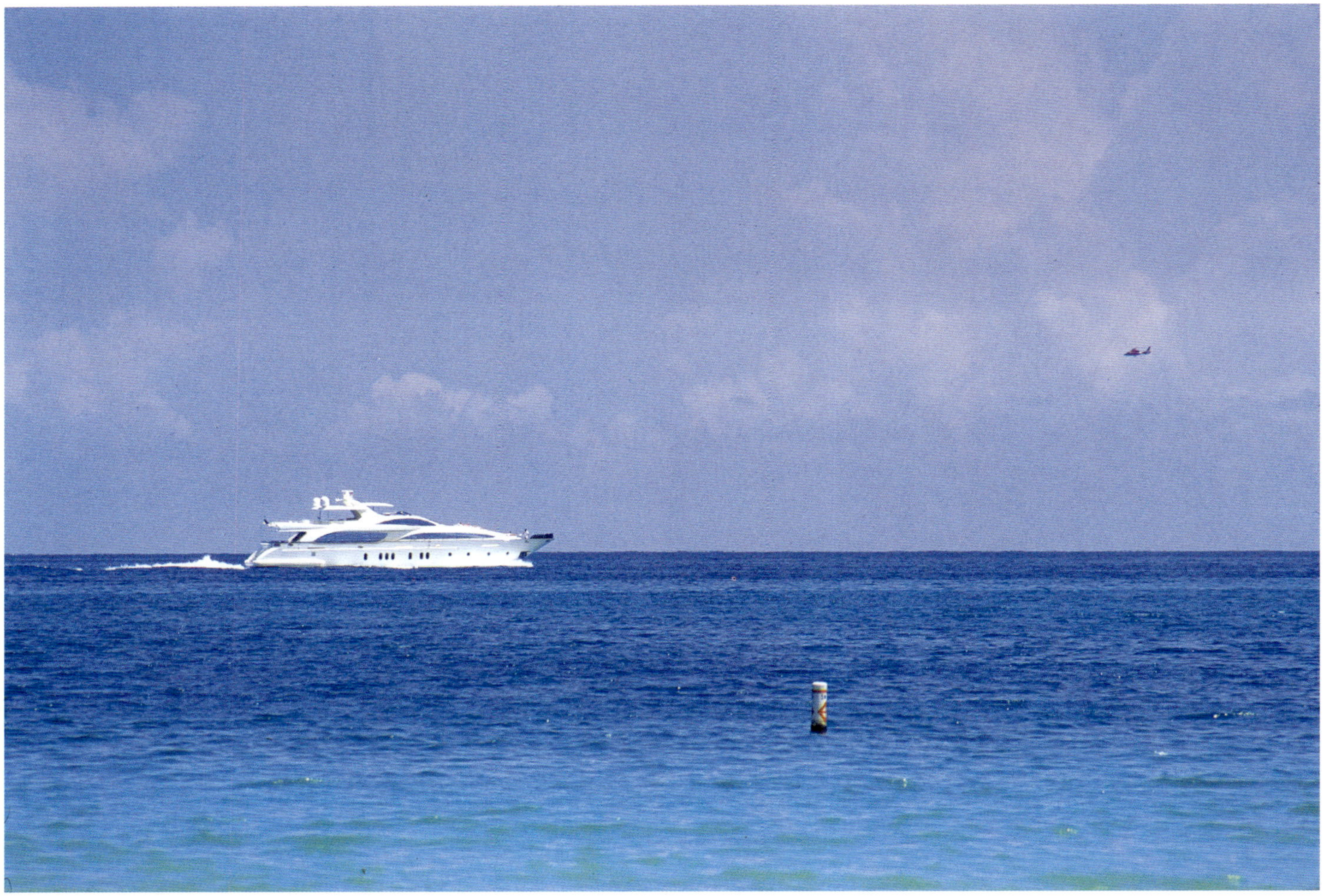

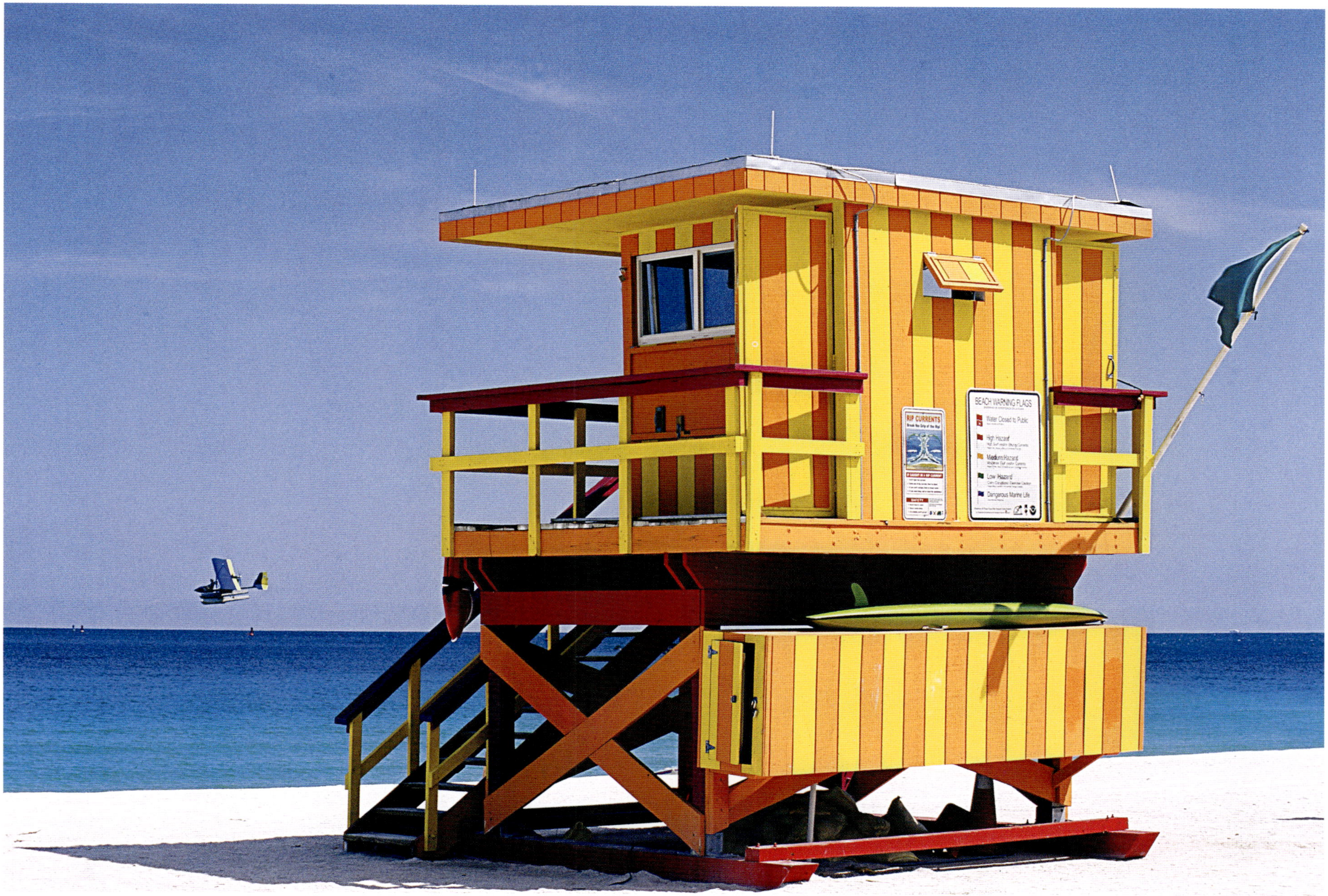
RIP CURRENTS
Break the Grip of the Rip!
BEACH WARNING FLAGS
Water Closed to Public
High Hazard
Medium Hazard
Low Hazard
Dangerous Marine Life

5ST Guardhouse

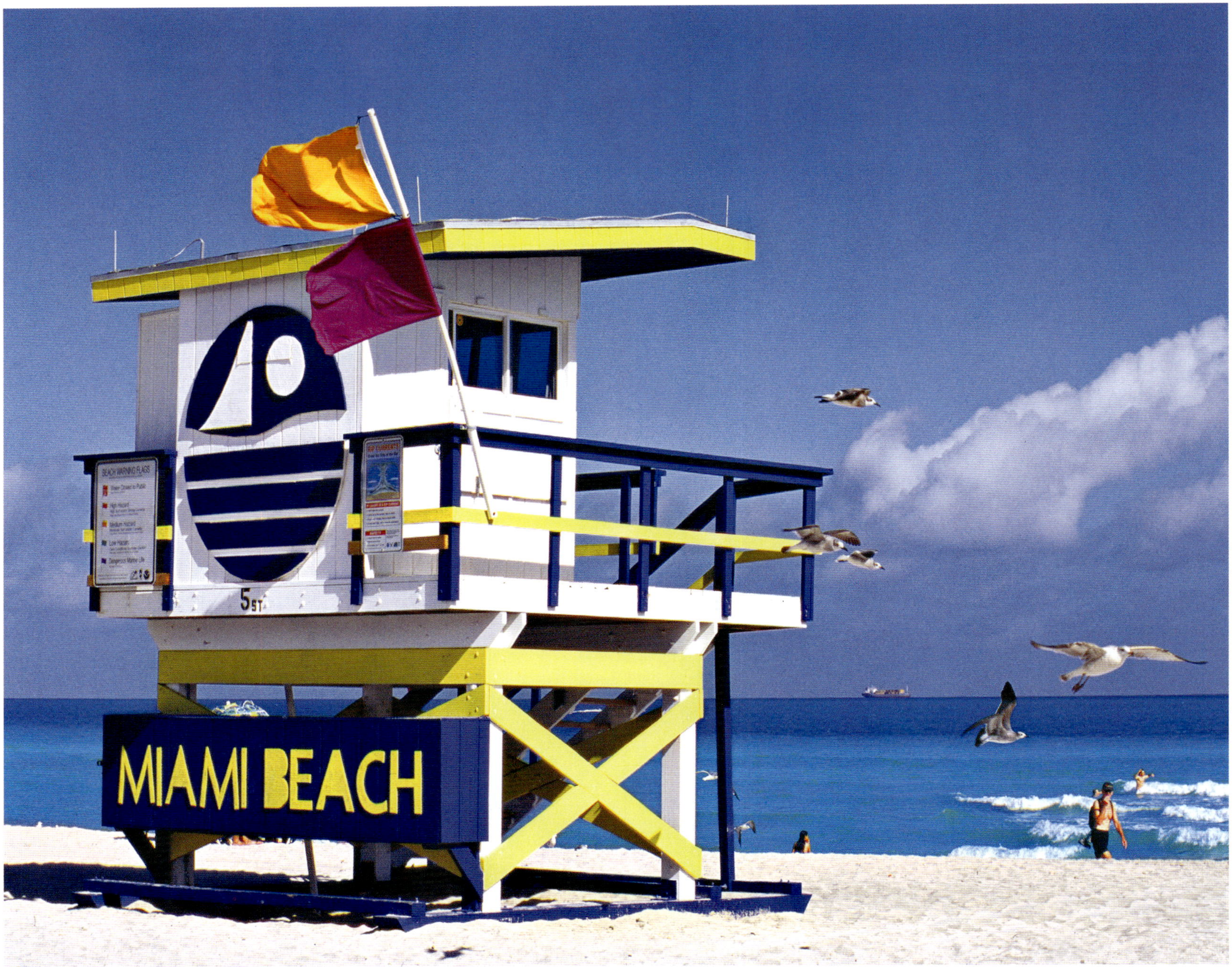

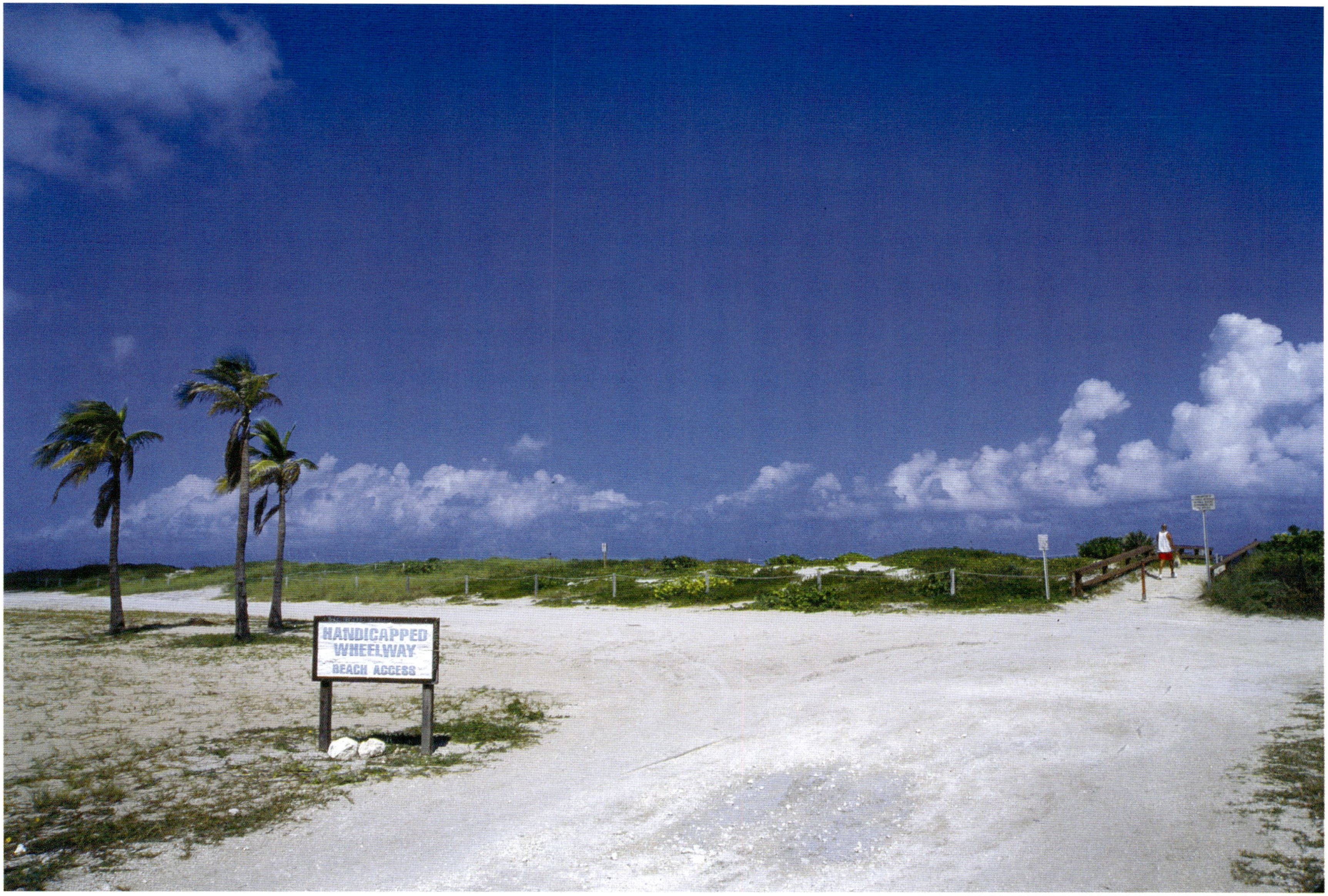

Here comes a very clever rendition of Miami Beach's official logo on a lifeguard station, cutouts of a sail, the sun, and the sea, decked out in bright yellow, navy blue, and brilliant white. Who could ask for anything more, and the multitudes of tourists and locals who wind up at the 5ST Guardhouse to have their pictures taken can attest to their choice of "one of the best."

On this January day, the yellow flag indicates a moderate surf or currents, and the purple banner warns of possible dangerous marine life. The lifeguard can explain any restrictions.

Located at the Fifth Street entrance, this beach access provides a "Handicapped Wheelway," which means the sand is more navigable and the ramp not steep. However, a sand wheelchair is still required to get all the way onto the beach. A few blocks away, at the Beach Patrol Headquarters on 10th Street, several special wheelchairs are available to use on a first-come, first-served basis. (Tel: 305-673-7714)

Fifth Street is also the beginning of beautiful Lummus Park that stretches north ten blocks, with the beach on one side and busy Ocean Drive on the other.

Old 6ST Guardhouse

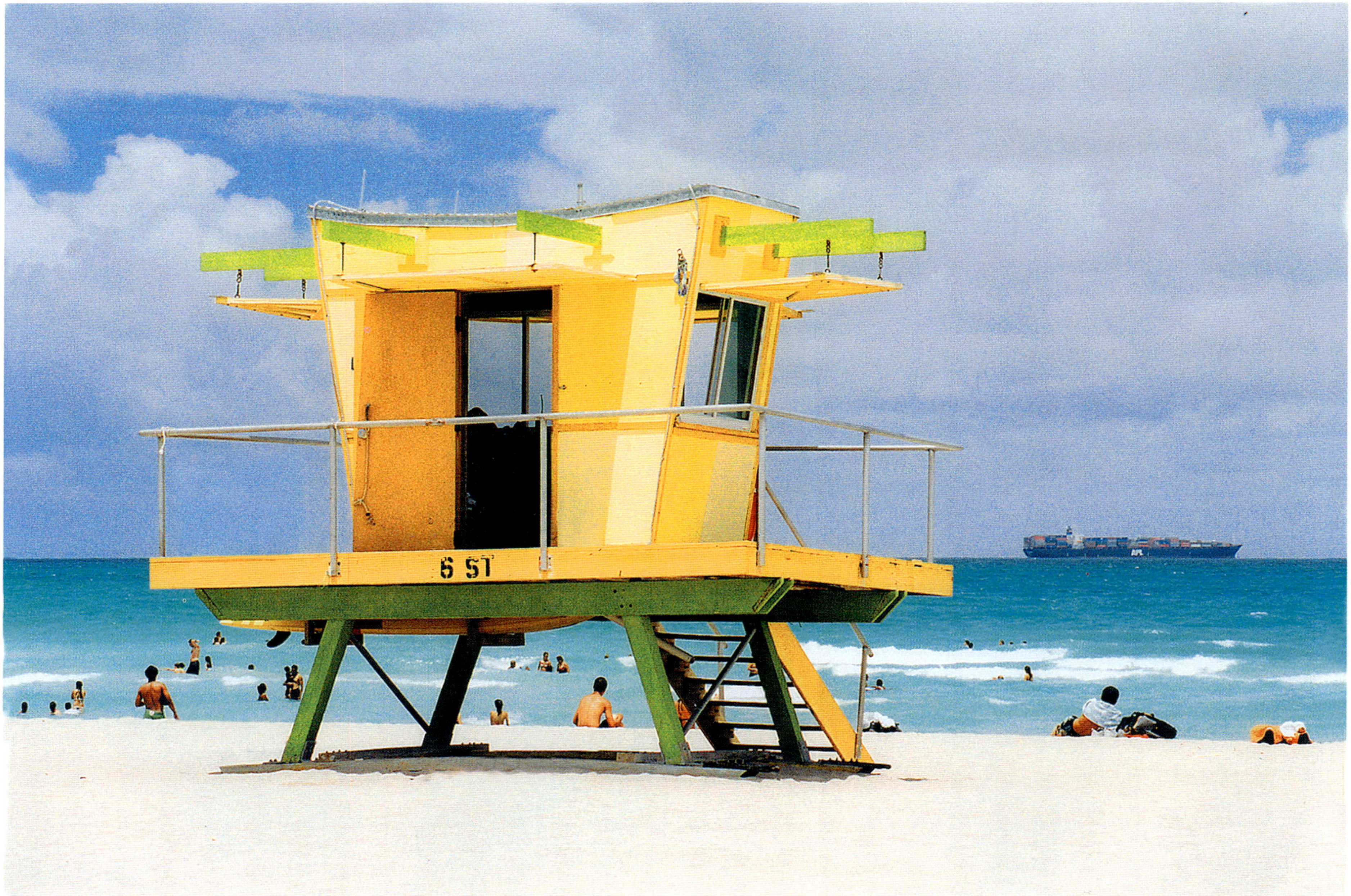

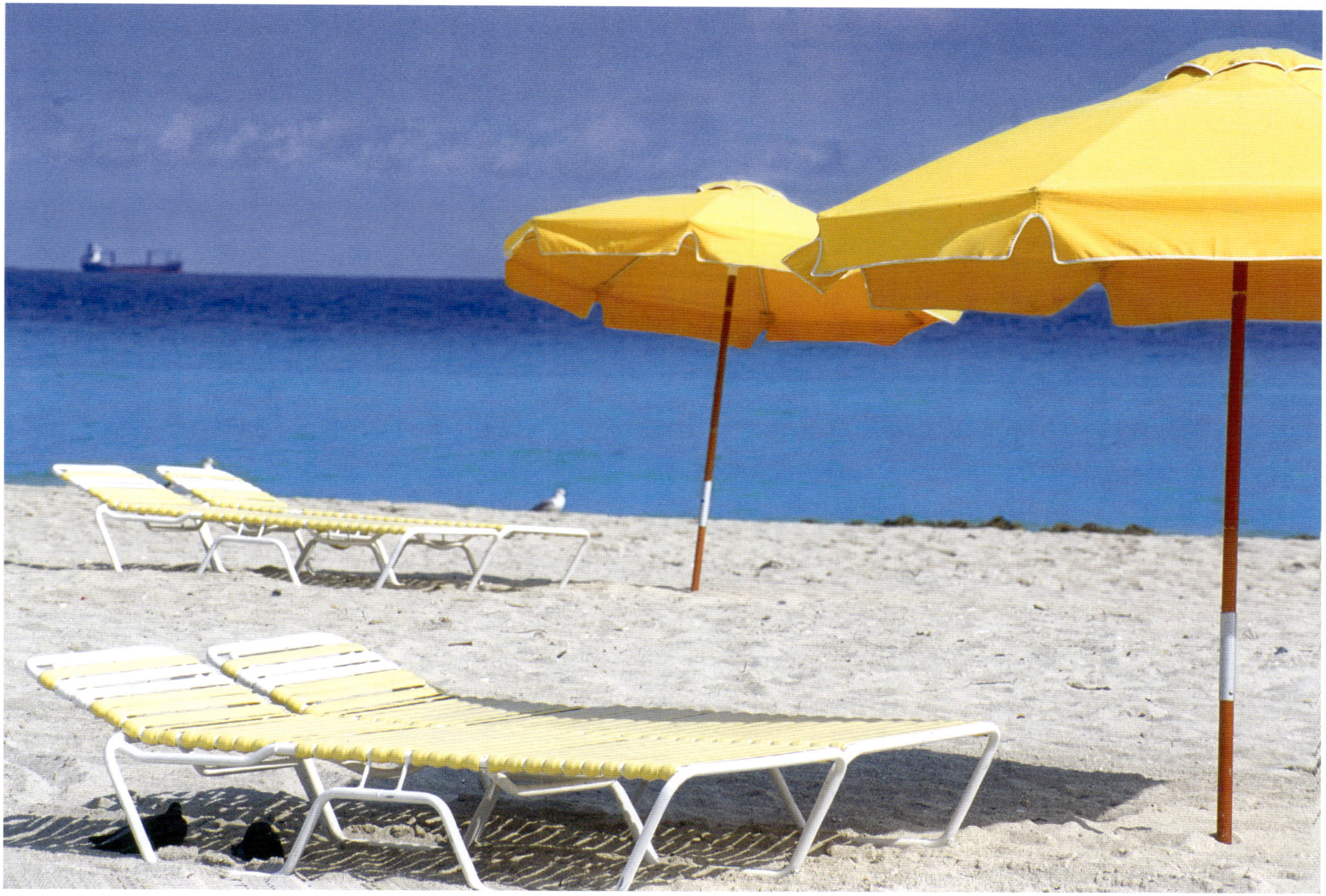

This whimsical yellow lifeguard station became the 6th Street Guardhouse after Hurricane Andrew, and stayed there for over ten years, until it was moved into one of the more northern areas of Miami Beach.

While it was tough enough to endure several strong storms, and charming enough to be called a delight, the design is not being duplicated because of a desire for guardhouses to stand a bit higher off the sand and have more convenient openings for windows. Nevertheless, it's been, and continues to be, a bright beacon on the sands of Miami Beach.

In the southern section of South Beach, near where the old guardhouse stood, is a large grouping of yellow umbrellas, a myriad of little golden sunbursts on the sand. There are yellow and white chaise lounges to match, and turquoise waters and blue skies to complete the mural. One set of four umbrellas is set aside as a play area for children, with a shallow pit dug out in the sand, surrounded by four tiny blue chairs and lots of beach toys.

Blue cabanas, small hutch-like shelters with air vents in the back, are available, too. The umbrellas, chaise lounges, and cabanas can all be rented.

6ST Guardhouse

Located between 6th and 7th streets, this charming lifeguard station combines the look of a Swiss chalet with its triple-peaked roof lines and little wooden children's toys of pickup sticks and puzzle pieces, attached as decorations. I call it "The Playhouse." Officially, it is the 6ST Guardhouse.

On the beach this October morning, it's an exquisitely calm day, and the beach is not yet crowded. It will become busier as the day wears on.

And now is a good opportunity to become familiar with certain regulations for beach use. One of the signs on a typical entryway instructs visitors about these basic rules, and a quick glance is in order before settling in on the sand for the day.

Your favorite dog has to stay home (and all animals), and alcohol is not allowed on the beach either. Glass containers and any other unsafe items are not permitted. The beach officially closes from midnight to 5 a.m. However, it should be noted that lifeguards are on duty from 9:30 a.m. until 6:30 p.m. for nine months of the year, and from 9:30 a.m. to 4:30 p.m. the remaining three winter months. It is always weather permitting, of course, because during dangerous thunderstorms or other serious weather events, guards will clear the water and close the beach.

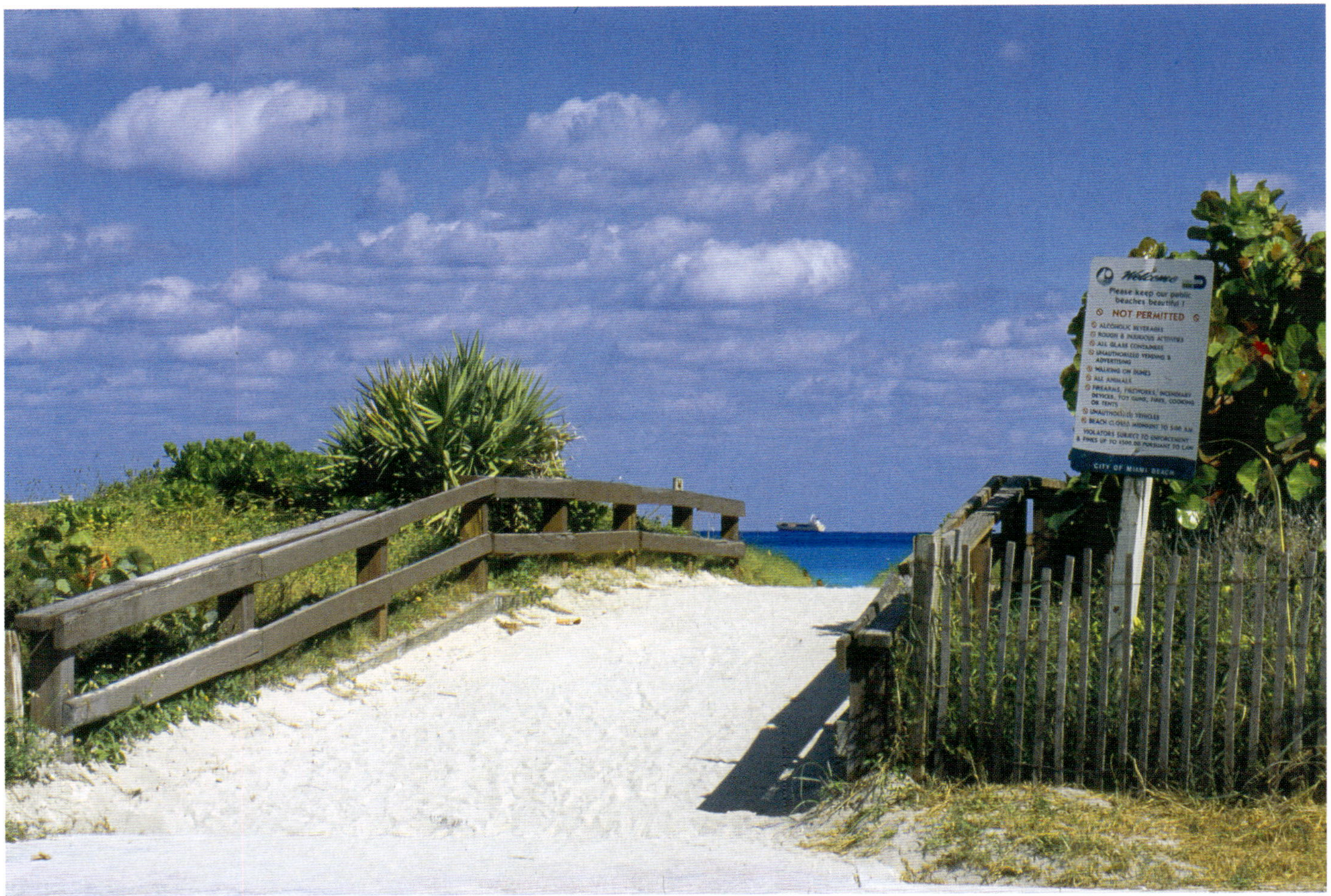

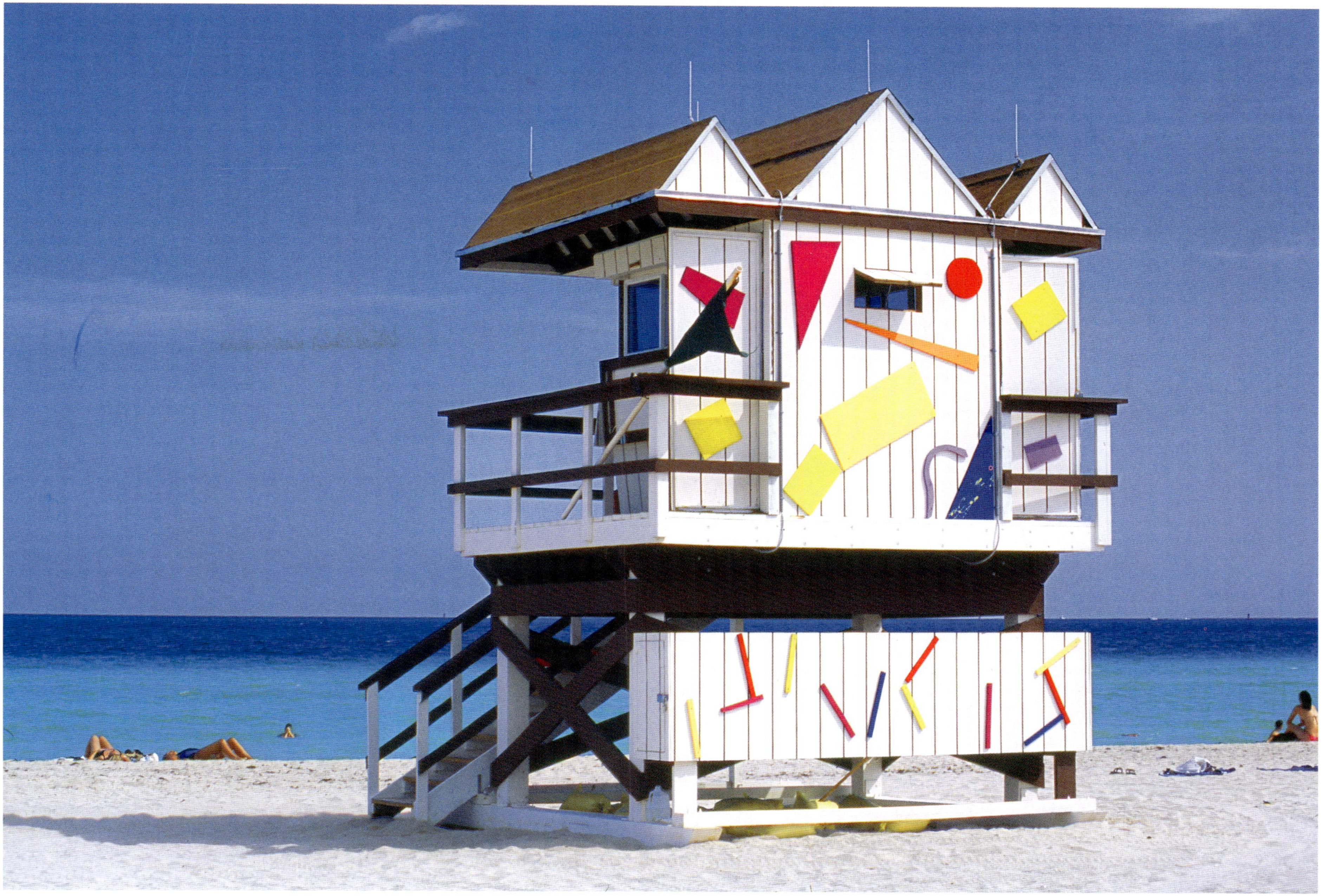

Old 8ST Guardhouse

This great guardhouse had everything it needed for it to be a perfect lifeguard station on South Beach: imaginative style, height, wonderful colors. Everything that is, but permanence. It went down in one of the hurricanes in the fall of 2005, and those pink, ribbon-like railing slats were lost forever. Nothing is left but the picture and the memories.

However, that deep aqua color on the base and trim has carried on as a primary South Beach paint choice, and it brightens this and many of the other outdoor showers up and down Lummus Park at major beach access points.

And, here, notice the tint of the South Beach sand, too, a uniform light color that changes under the hues of dawn or dusk. It can go from grey to pink, but a warm tan is its real shade. It's not a sugary sand or soft like flour or rough like shells, although you will find some small shells embedded here and there. It's a sand with texture.

If you've got some in your shoes, shake it out. If there's sand on your feet, rinse it off at the shower station, and catch a drink at the water fountain while you're at it.

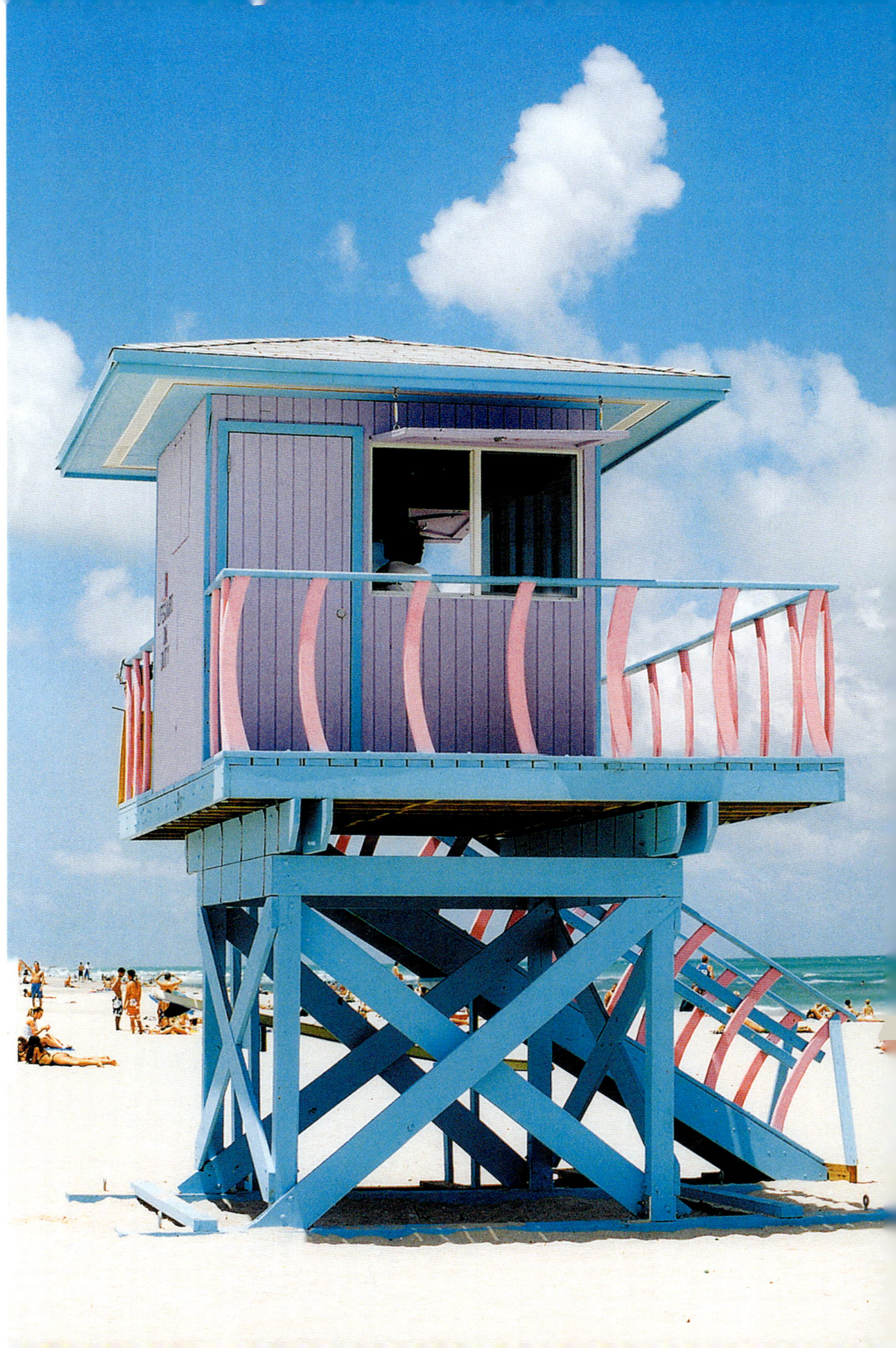

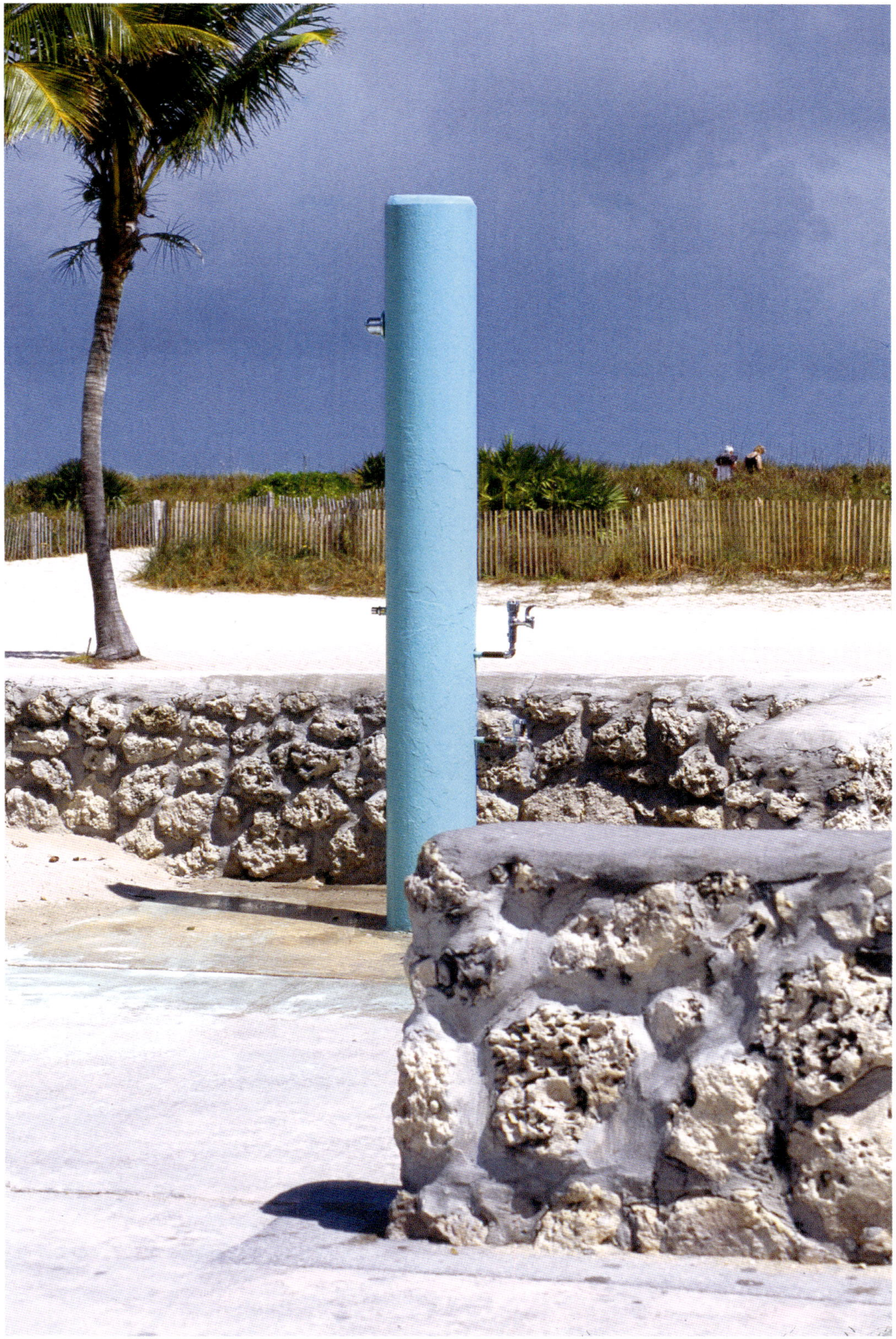

8ST Guardhouse

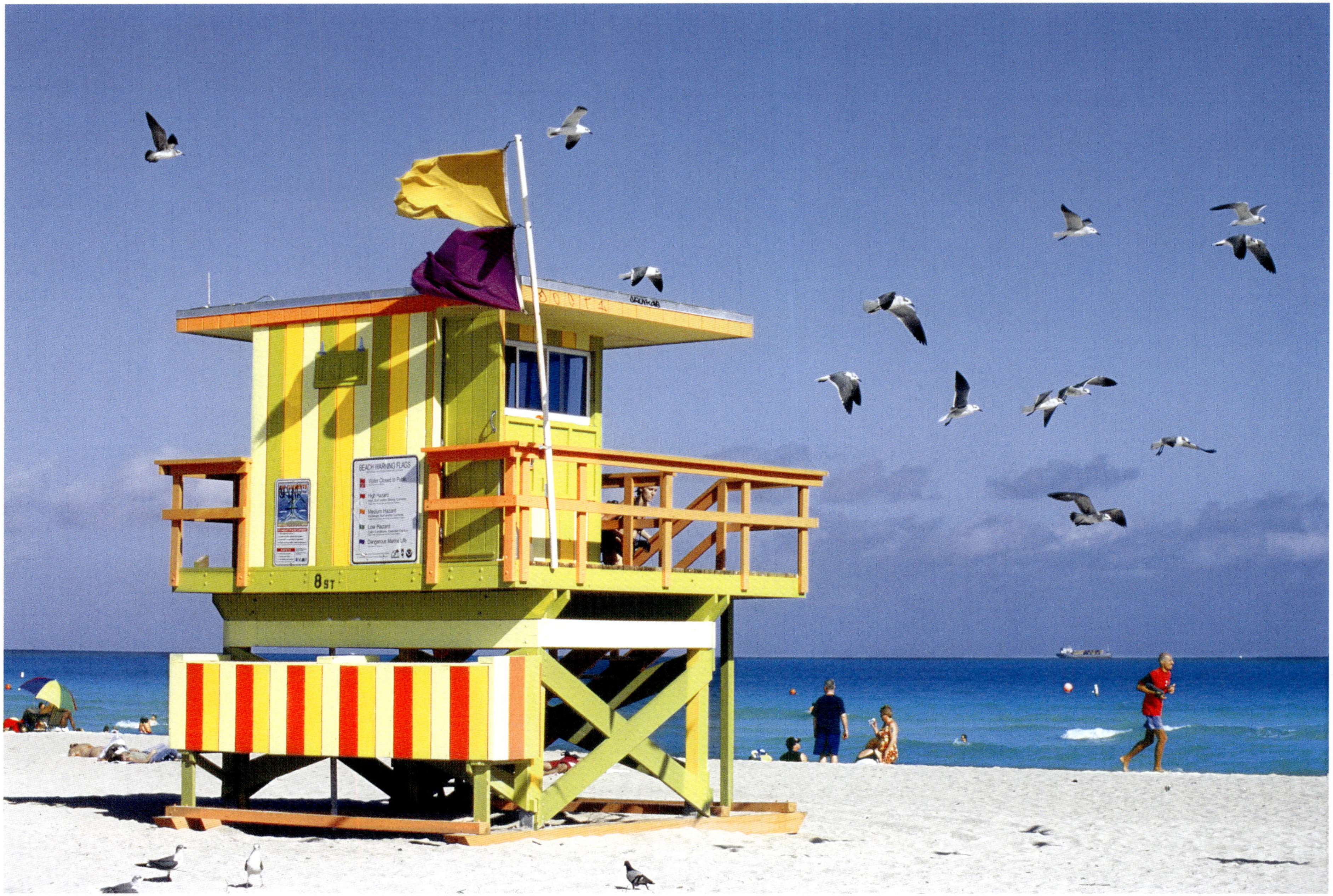

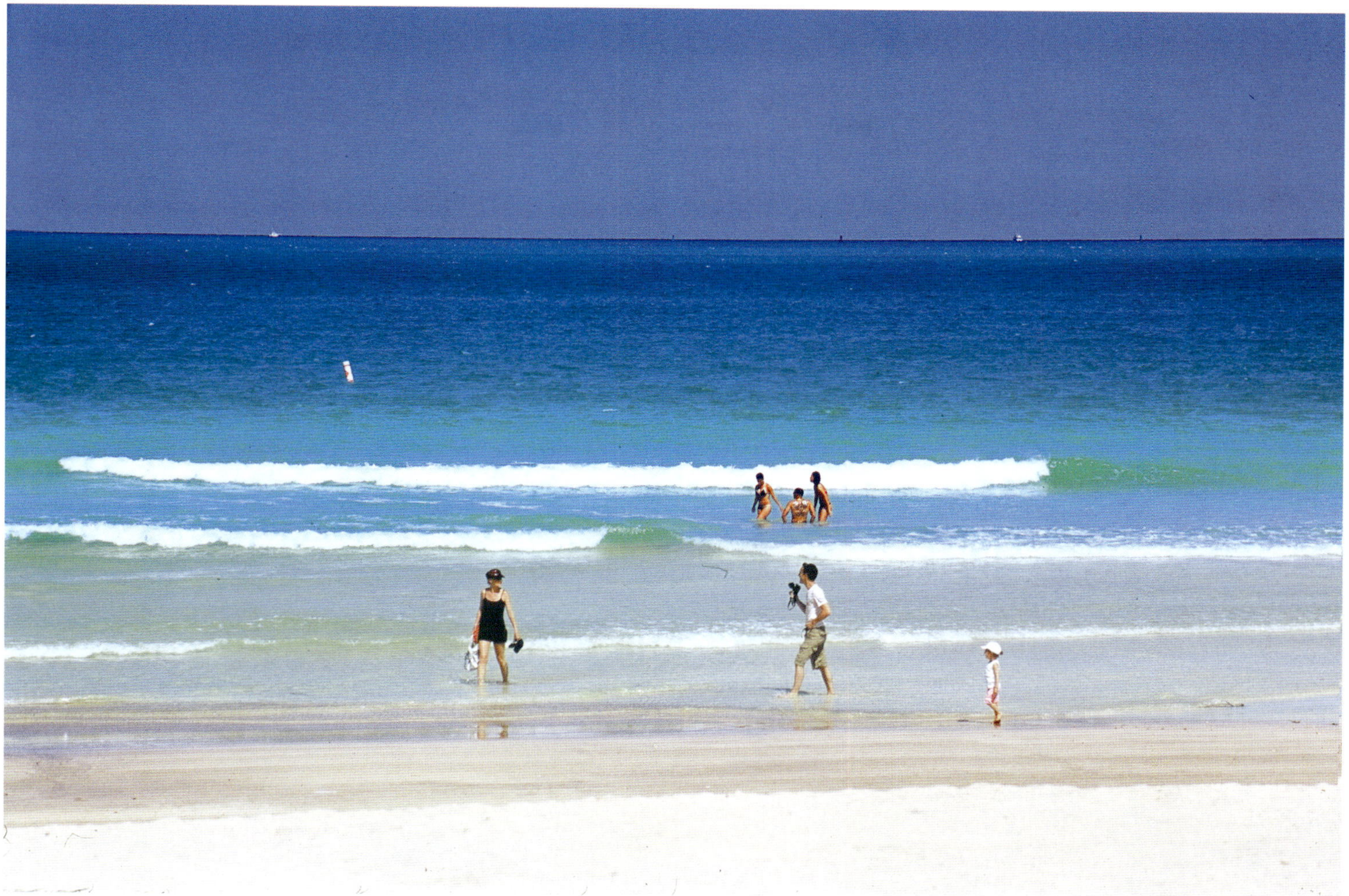

Seagulls are all aflutter around this new 8ST Guardhouse, a bright complexion of oranges, yellows, and pale greens. Warning flags fly on this January afternoon, but it is a beach draw, nevertheless, with warm breezes and nearly clear skies. Cooler waters than summertime don't deter the swimmers, especially those from the North, who think of it as bath water compared to the cold lakes and rivers they are used to.

Runners find the beach a perfect place to jog and families are often out with their cameras to catch a ship on the horizon, or each other in the lens.

A second visit months later in June came under darkening skies, with a dangerous summer tropical storm building over the Atlantic waters to the east and almost surrounding the beach area to the west and north.

As a chilled wind began blowing, lifeguards up and down the beach sprang into action, signaling swimmers out of the water and into a safe haven, which was off the beach entirely. When the swimmers were gone, the guards were picked up by supervisors and transported to their Beach Patrol Headquarters on 10th Street to wait out the storm.

A short time later, the storm was gone and life resumed on the beach, just as always.

10ST Guardhouse

This is the most famous lifeguard stand on South Beach! Its totally round architecture a la spaceship, a la ship's turret, a la magical antenna, a la bubblegum-hue cum sock-it-to-the-eyes yellow, defies an exact description, except to say it has graced many a book and magazine cover, not to mention its stardom on TV and in the movies. Conceived by noted architect William Lane and renowned artist Kenny Scharf, it went up after Hurricane Andrew and has stood the test of time through more than its share of inclement weather.

Beautiful Lummus Park continues along this trek, with the guardhouse a peek in the distance, this time a pale pink, a perfect match to the park sign on this particular March day, several years ago. The lush park is filled with palm trees and other vegetation, colorful chairs and benches, grass that invites one to lie on it – and next to a low coral rock wall, a curving cementway that can be skated on, run on, strolled on.

One can perch on the low wall or on one of the benches and watch the sights go by. And there are sights that go by! Every kind of wild "do," showoff skaters, swim suits of greater or lesser material, guitar players, card players, games players.

Families from every part of the world will be speaking languages you've never heard. Tall people, short people, kids laughing and running. A great collage of humanity, all on South Beach seeking that "it factor" they've heard so much about.

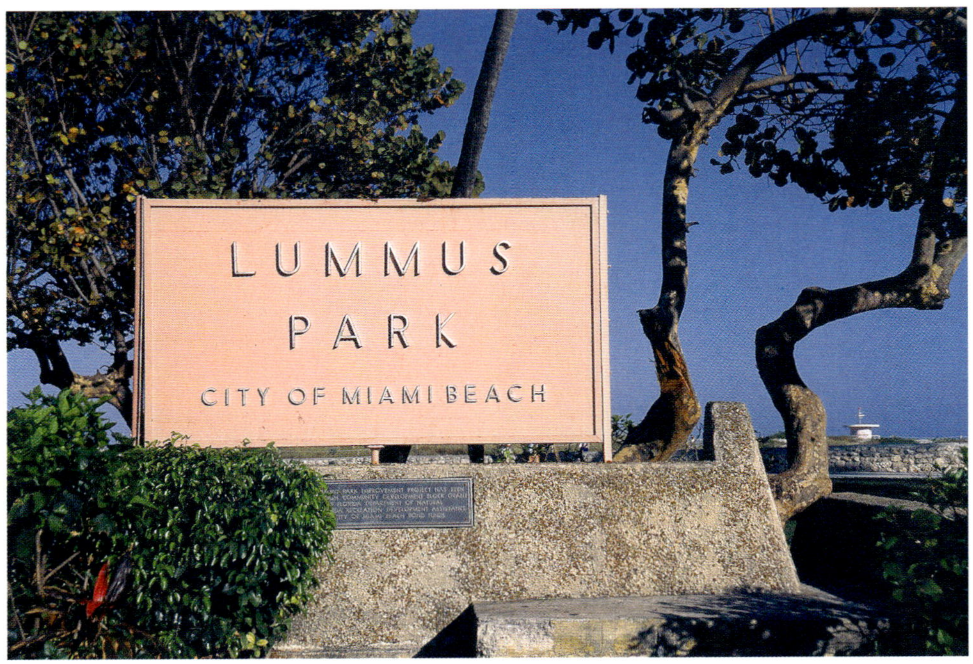

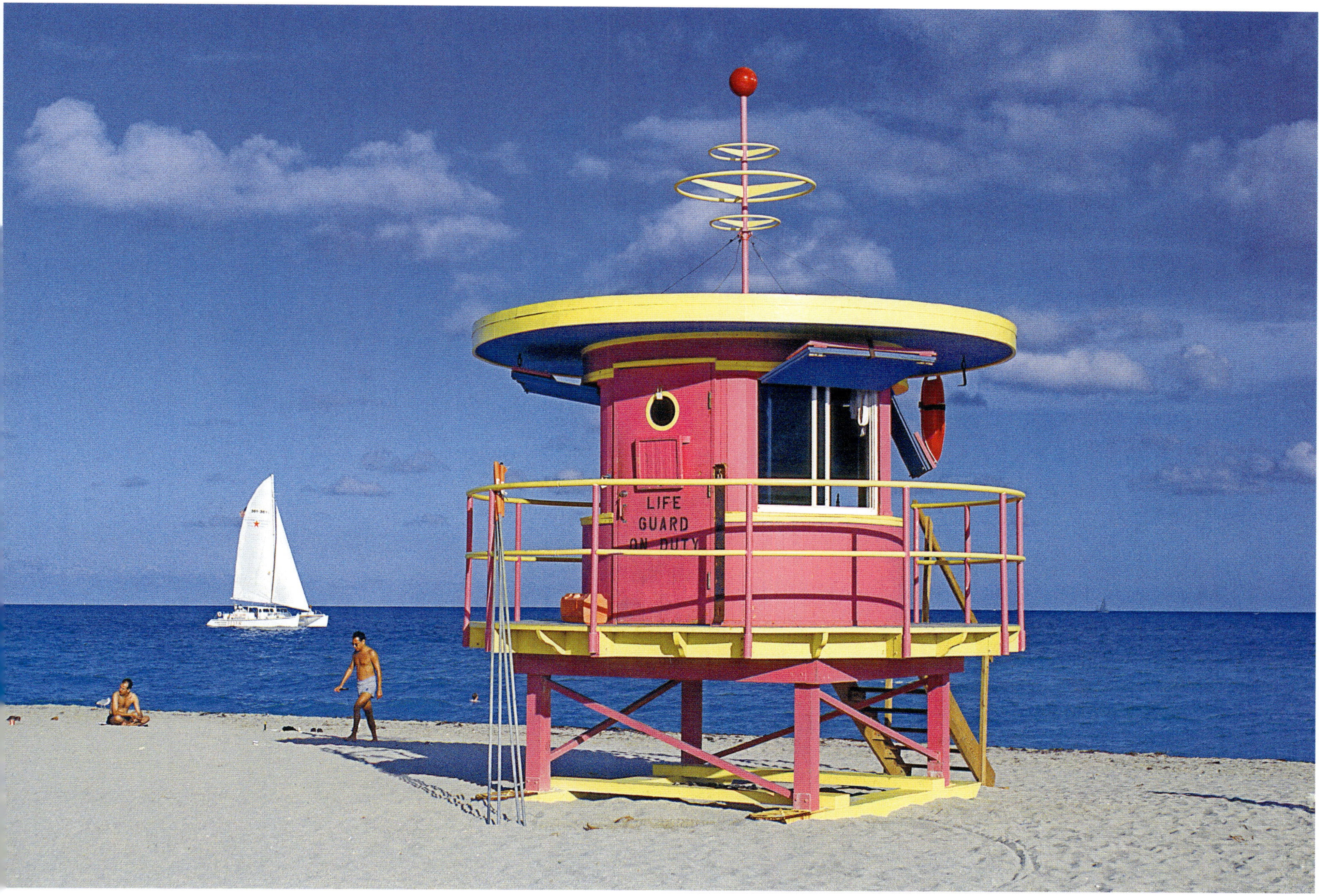
LIFE
GUARD
ON DUTY

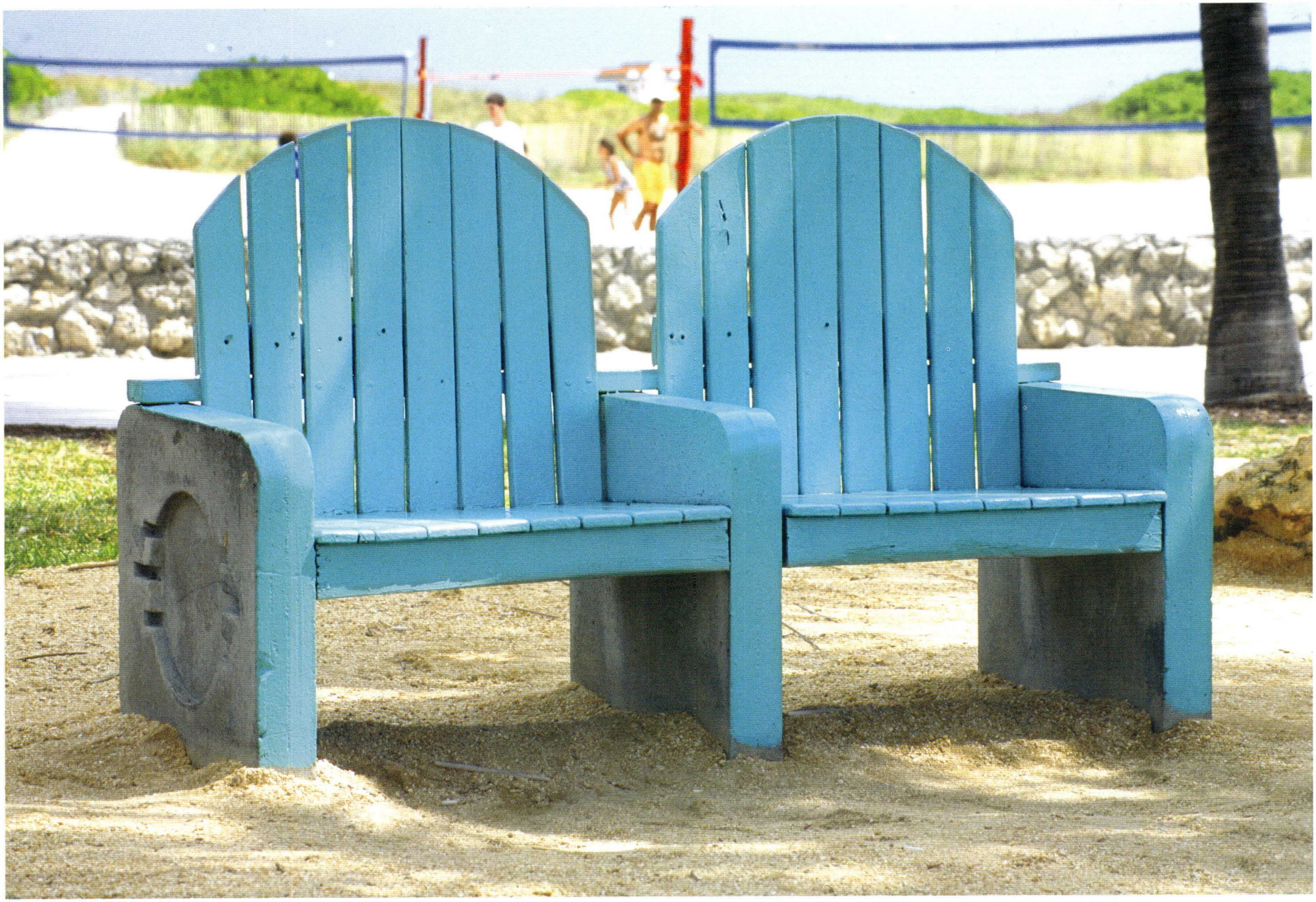

Nautical Art Deco is appropriately the style of this 1930s Beach Patrol Headquarters on 10th Street and Ocean Drive, facing the ocean. It's where the offices are for the Miami Beach Ocean Rescue Division and where wheelchair users can borrow the several beach access chairs, available on a first-come, first-served basis. (Tel: 305-673-7714).

The headquarters building has renovations on its schedule in the coming months. They will provide more room and better access, but will not alter the historic nature of this famous nautical gem. On this May day, the Beach Patrol Headquarters looked picture perfect.

Dubbing these lawn-type, old-fashioned chairs "South Beach Aqua," this pair was photographed closer to the 8th Street Guardhouse, but they are to be found everywhere near the beach and in the park. Made of wood and concrete and often in pairs or triples, they can't be easily moved or tipped over. Stretching out on them is not exactly a comfortable option, but there's always the inviting grass under a palm tree.

Doesn't that sound like a tropical dream scene?

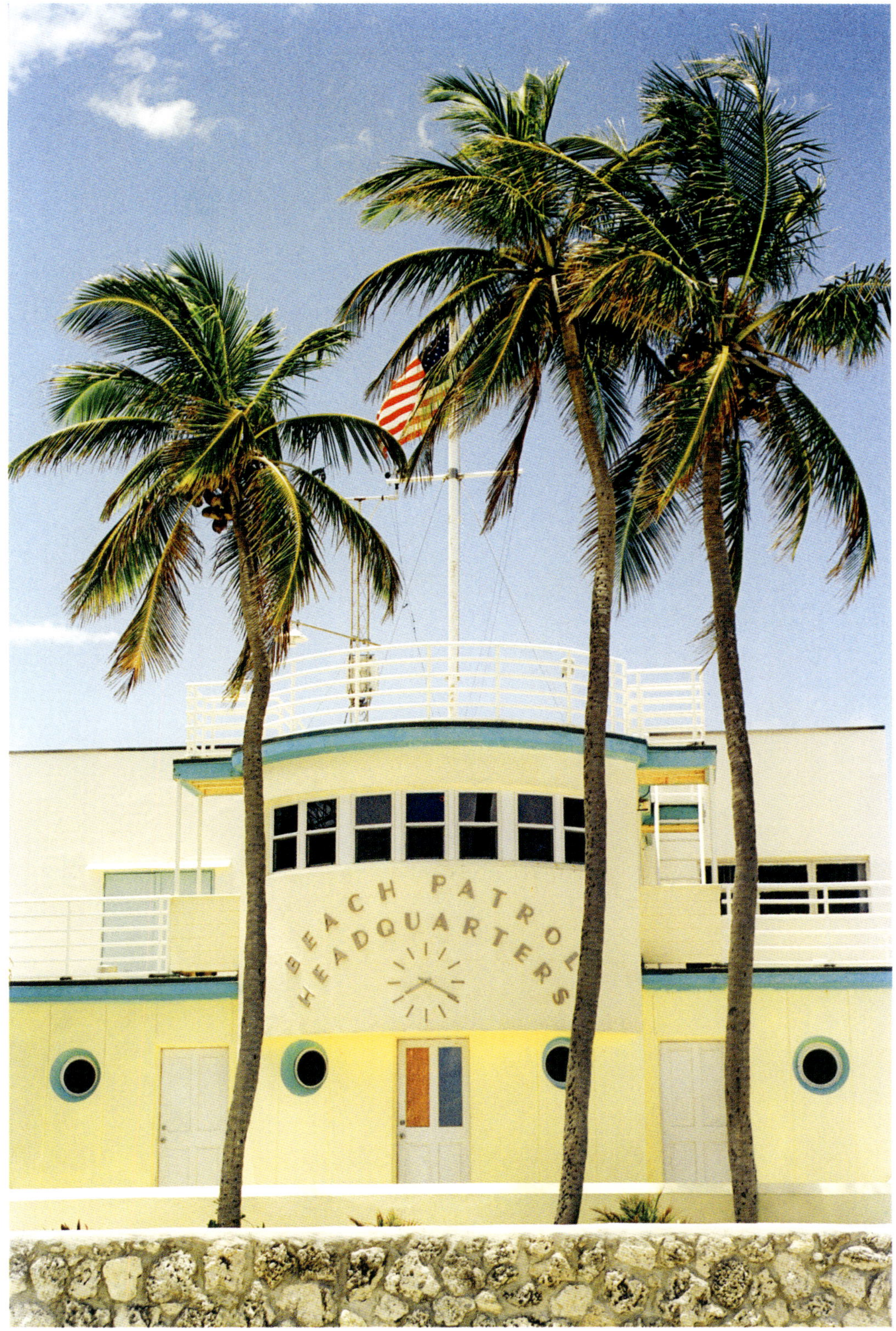

Miami Beach Date and Temperature Monument

Still close to 10th Street, you'll find this Miami Beach Date and Temperature Monument just steps from the street-side of the Beach Patrol building, which is the Ocean Drive headquarters for the Miami Design Preservation League offices and gift shop. The shop is a source of great Deco information, walking tours, and, of course, books and souvenirs.

The location also has the privilege of being a part of South Beach's often busiest corner, 10th Street and Ocean Drive.

The temperature on this day in March was an ideal 84 degrees. Summertime can get a little toasty, but delightful ocean waters and cool drinks can keep the heat at bay.

Near the monument are placards honoring the military who served during World War II on Miami Beach, a region which played an important role because of its strategic coastline.

Next stop: this pretty palm tree in the sand, which might not give all the shade that's needed, but the park just steps away has all the shade anyone could want.

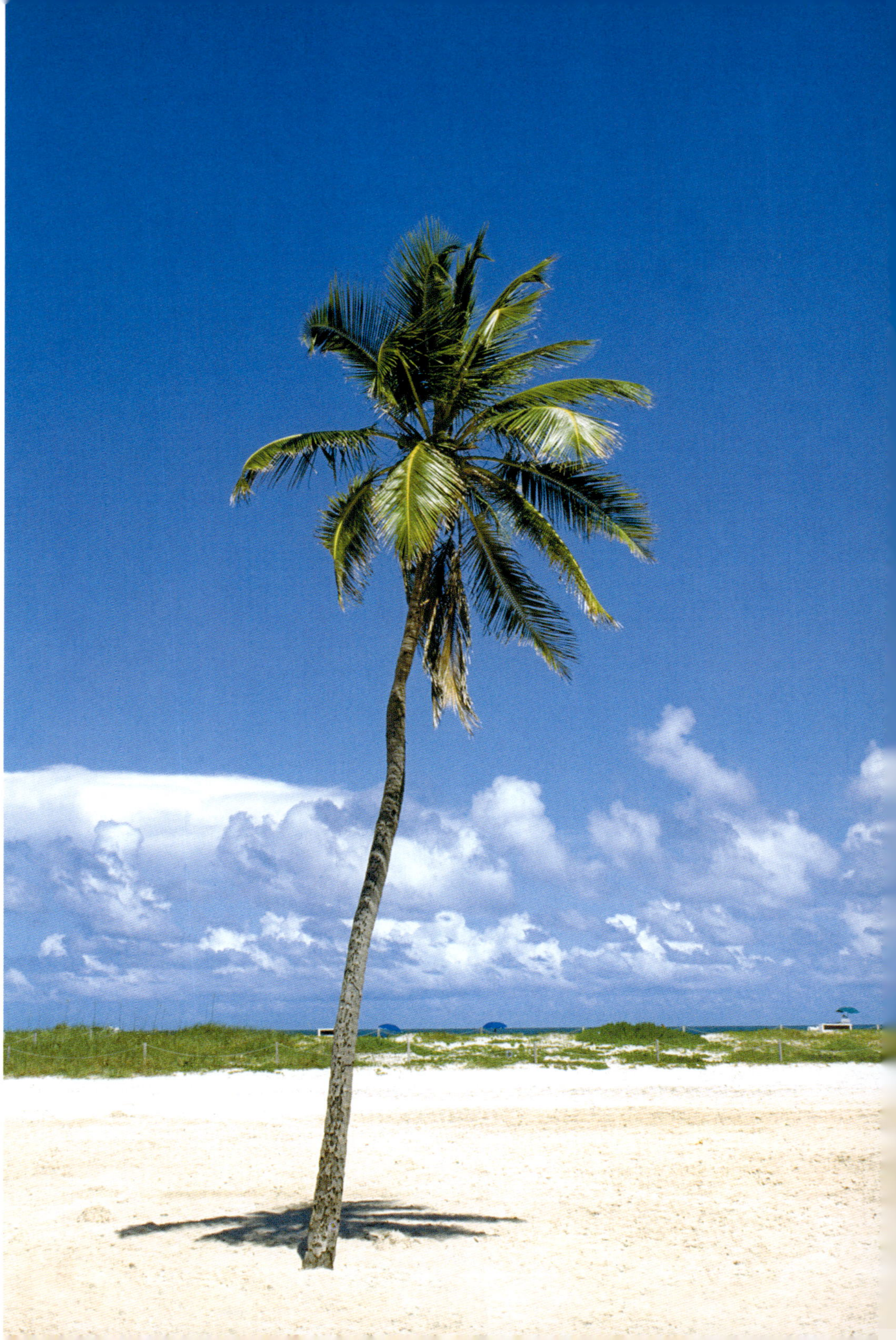

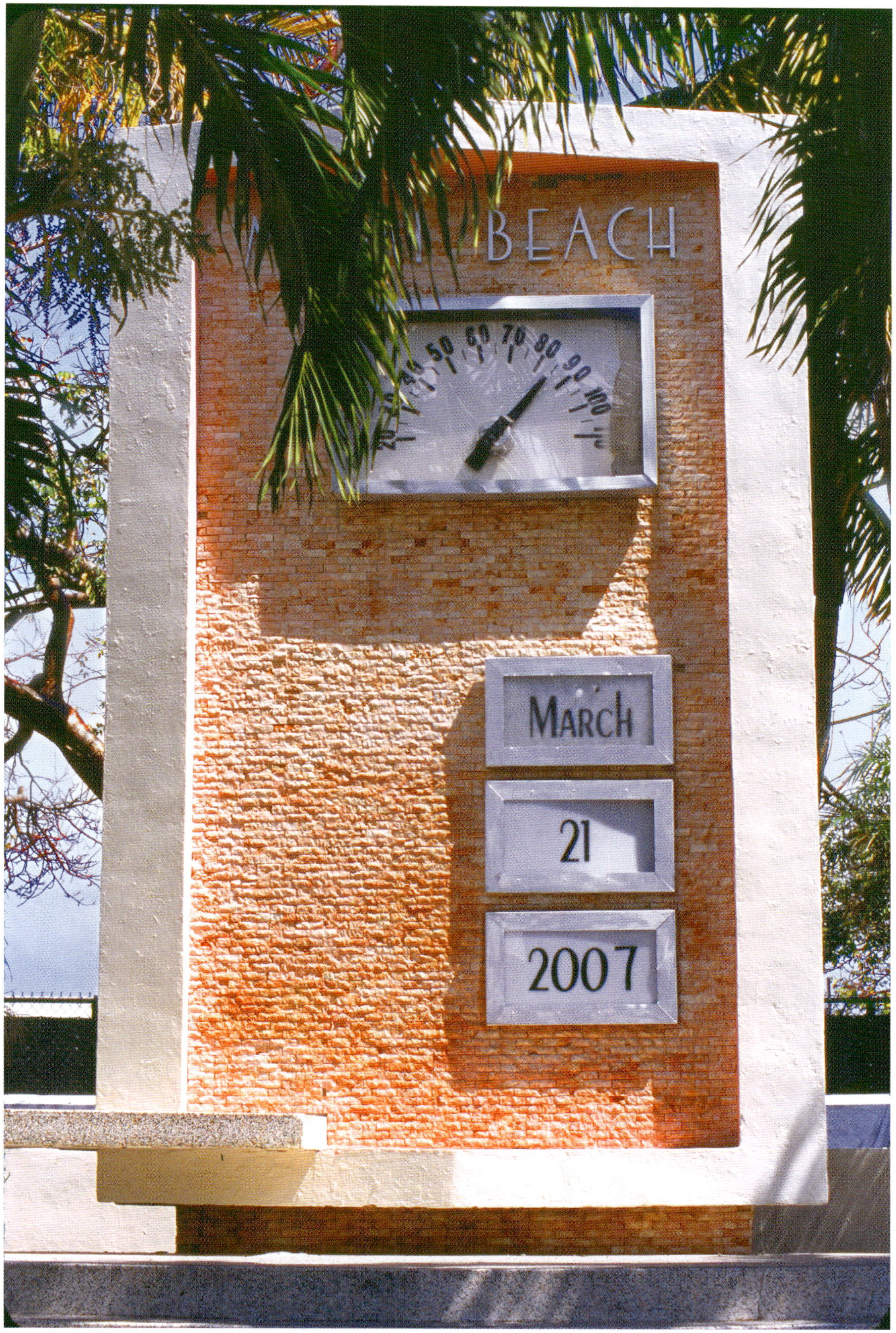
BEACH
March
21
2007

12ST Guardhouse

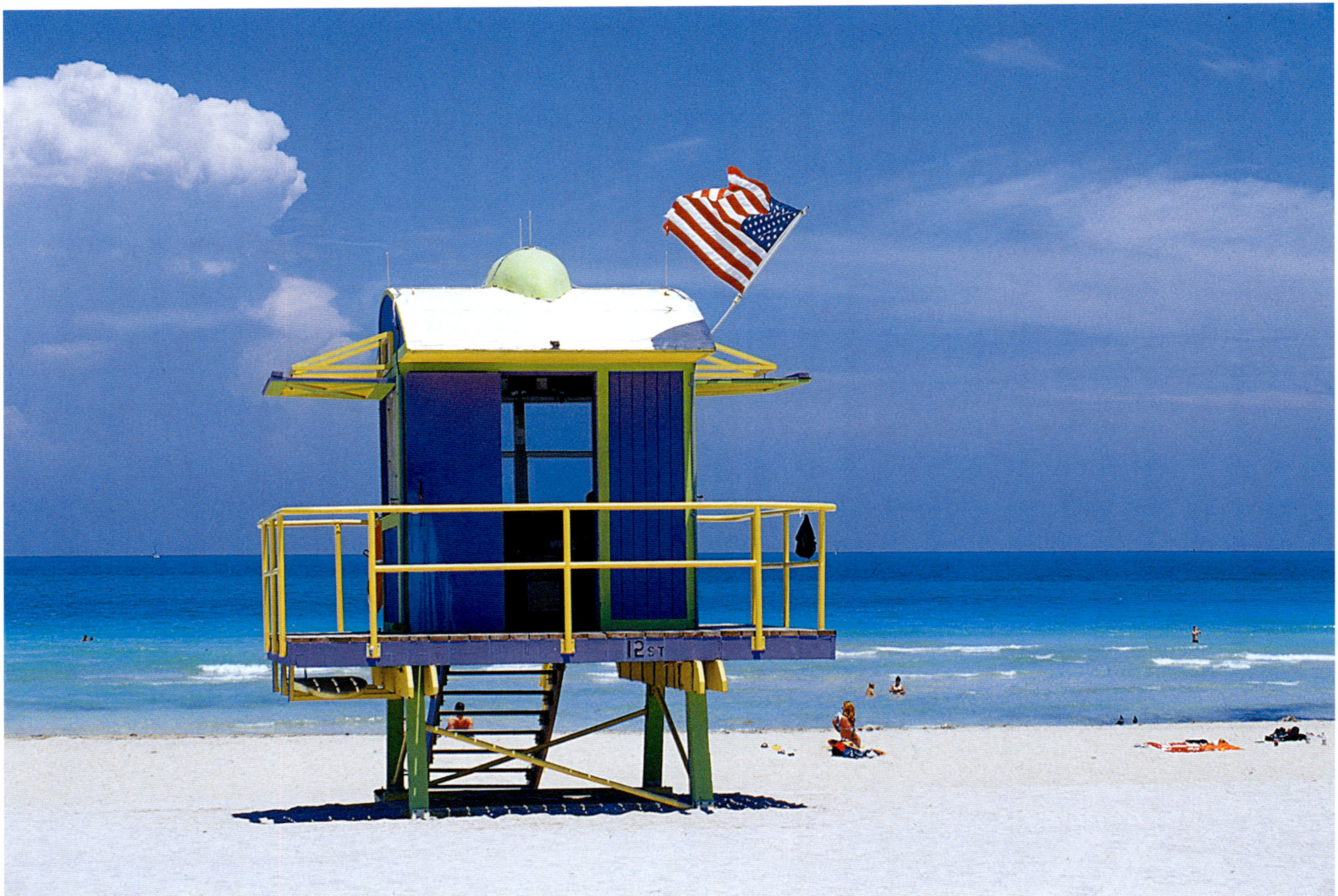

Hurricane Andrew's rebuilding brought this little purple guardhouse to life on the 12th Street beach, and neither rain nor wind of subsequent hurricanes could bring it down. Once called "The Duck," it stands where it always has, its curved roof with a topknot, providing a lookout for the lifeguards who watch over the swimmers at this busy locale off the northern reaches of Ocean Drive.

Famous Art Deco hotels and restaurants abound in this area, as well as it being home to the nearby former Versace mansion.

The beautiful 12th Street beach becomes as crowded or not as other prime shore destinations along Ocean Drive, depending on the season, the time of day, the day of the week, and the weather. This June afternoon was perfect in every way, with just enough breeze to keep the sunbathers comfortable.

It's the kind of day where a long walk along the shoreline in the gentle surf provides just the right dose of exercise, or floating on a board or noodle lulls a swimmer almost to sleep.

The other delightful alternative is to rent an umbrella (or unfurl your own), pull out your towel and a good book, and settle down for a few hours of complete relaxation.

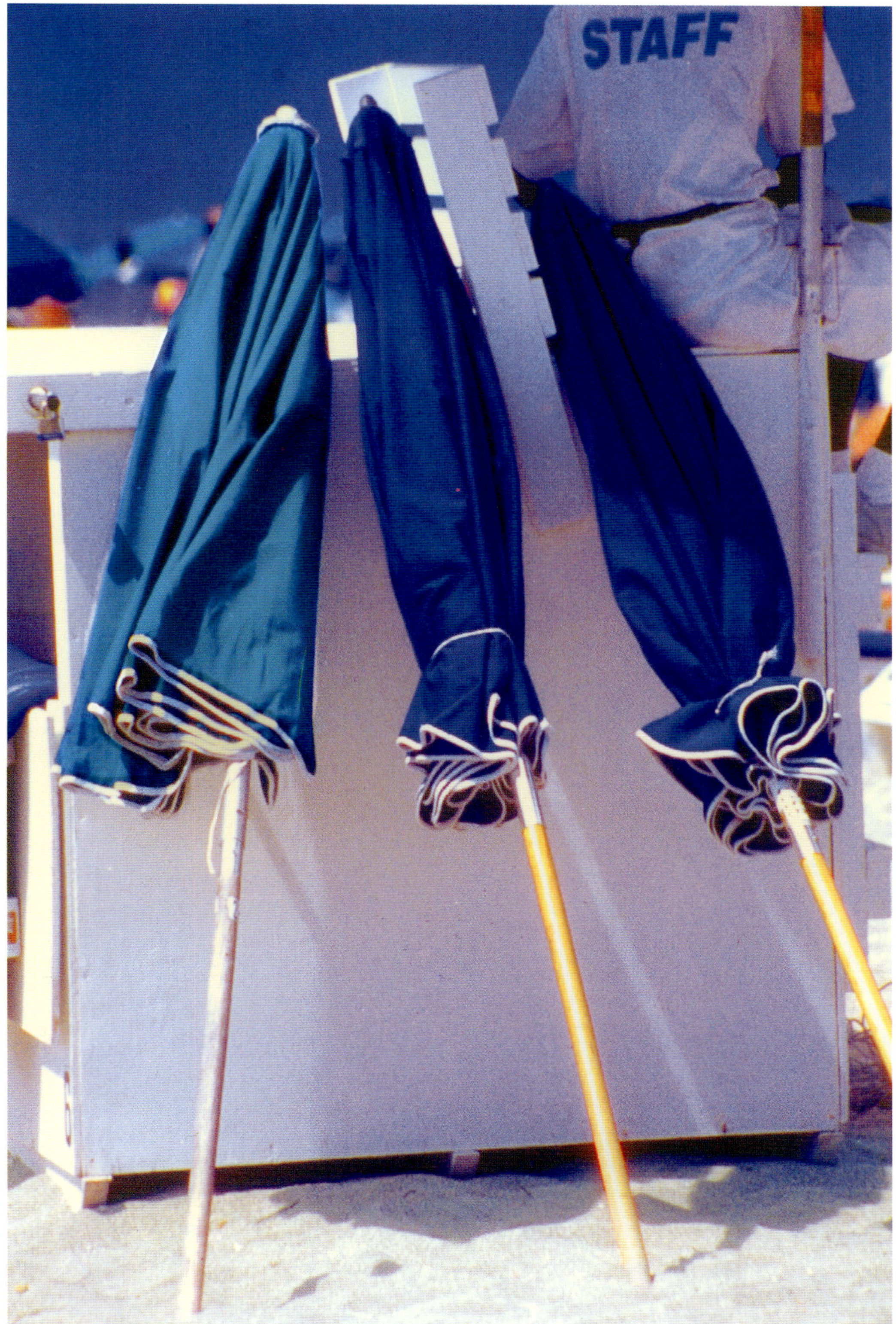

Old 13ST Guardhouse

Perhaps more than any other guardhouse lost in the storms of 2005, this one on 13th Street is the most lamentable. Commonly called "The Bed," it incorporated aspects of Turkish minarets and imaginative wooden detail both in cuts and angles of boards. The paint colors were carnival lavender, white, and that delicious bubblegum pink, with a gold frilly garland thrown in for good measure.

The 13th Street Guardhouse truly was both remarkable and outrageous and on this particular June day, a sight to behold. One could only circle around it again and again, seeking an angle to photograph that would not only get it all in, but do this gadfly justice. It was a day in paradise, one never to be forgotten.

Looking north from that sight and from almost any other spot on the beach, one takes in the curve of the seashore with its turquoise waters, foamy, gentle waves, and the elegant skyline of the preserved Art Deco buildings with the many new condominiums surrounding them.

South Beach is a world-class destination and its popularity shows no sign of waning, with visitors returning multiple times from every state in the union and nearly every country on the globe.

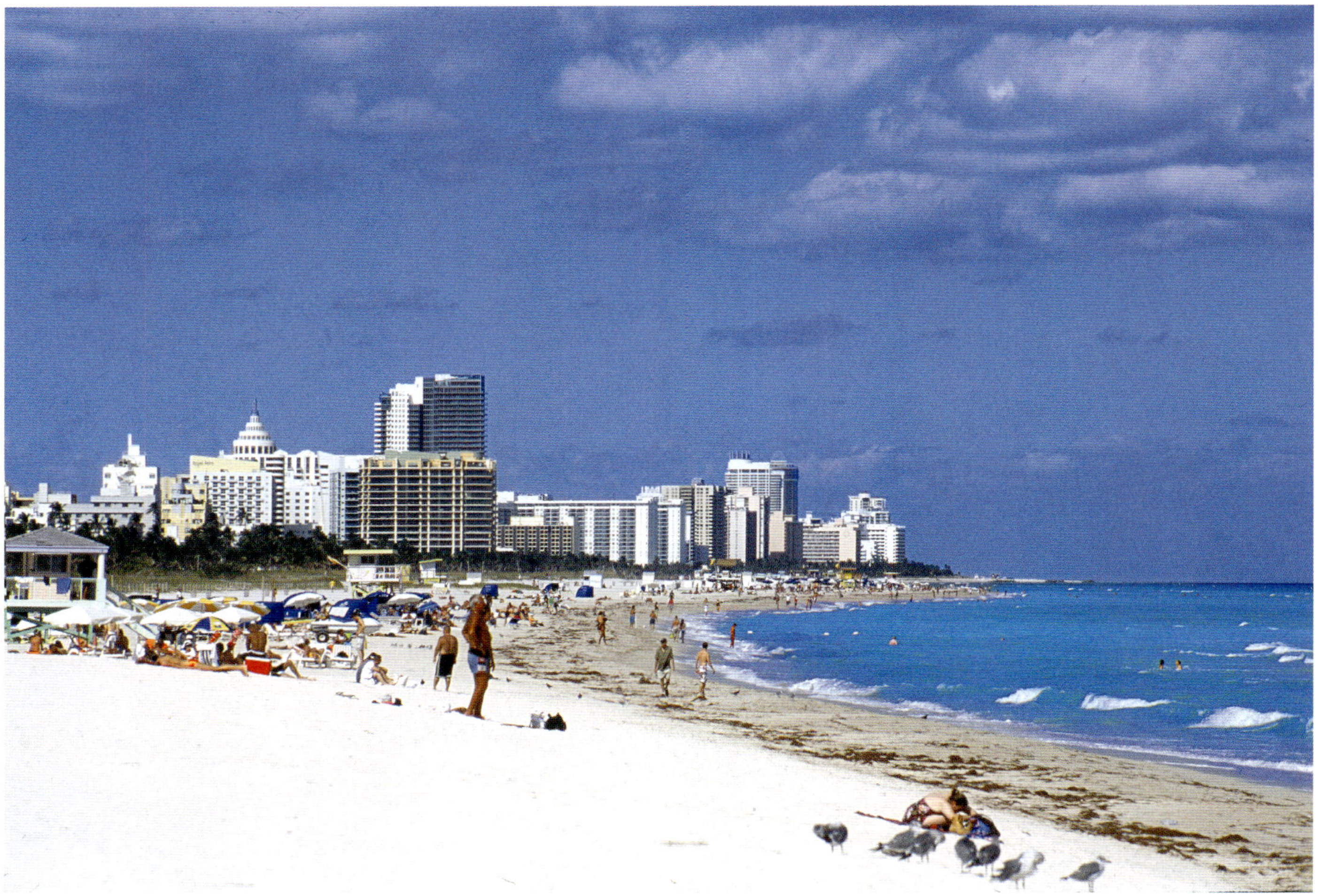

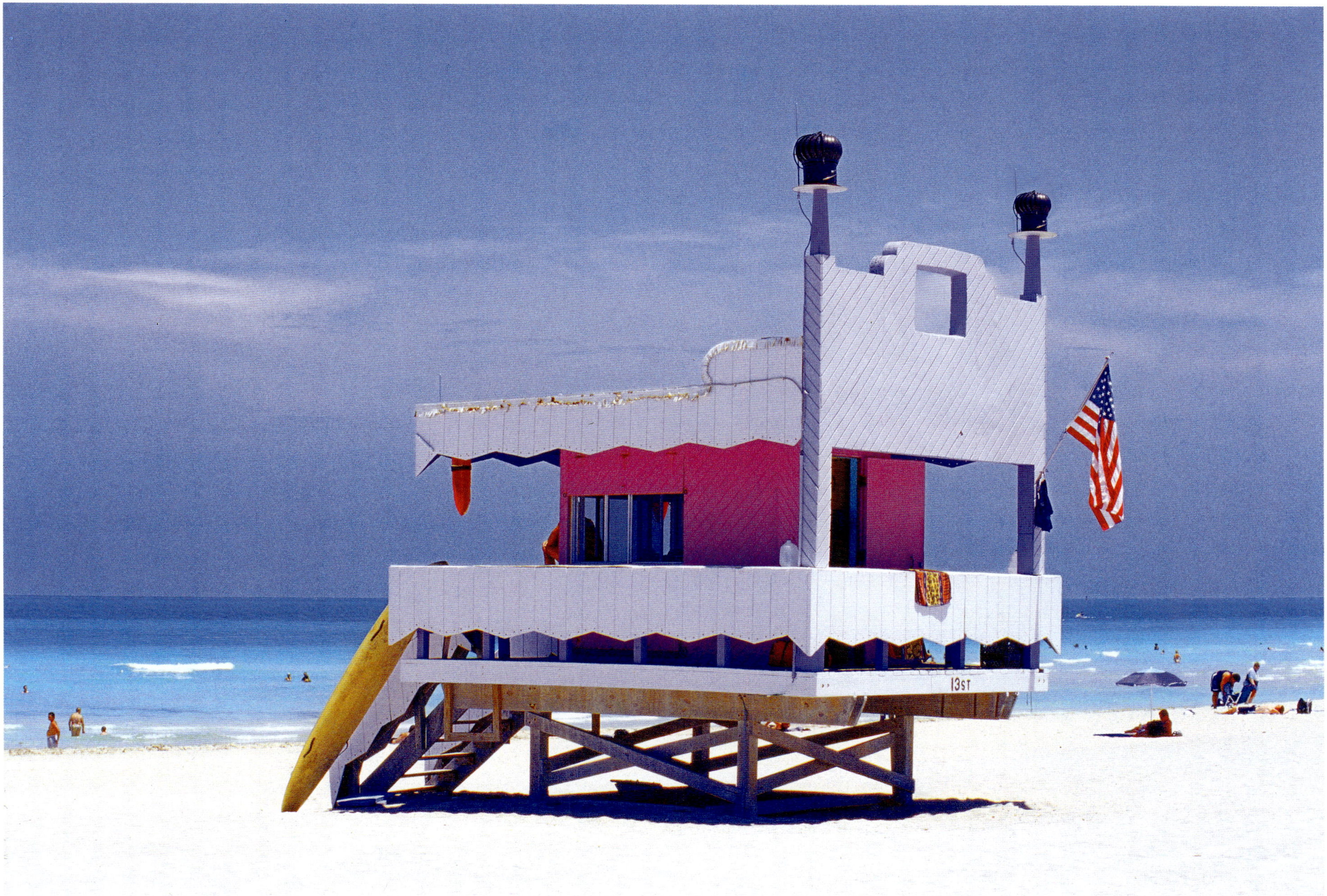
13ST

13ST Guardhouse

"Proud to be an American," shouts the new 13th Street lifeguard station, which also flew the U.S. flag on this sunny June afternoon for its portrait sitting. Picture-perfect seas invited swimmers to loll in the warm Atlantic waters, while a parasailor floats by for a wind-cooling, bird's-eye view of the sea, seashore, and Art Deco cityscape up and down the coastline.

The parasailor reported a breathtaking view, an easy and exciting adventure, and an experience to be repeated at the first opportunity.

But, whoa! Who are these tourists sitting on the South Beach sands? Looks like they are having a very animated discussion, and there is no equivocation about the nationality they are claiming.

But it's safe to say they are content where they are, spending their vacation money on American soil, and not looking like they are in any hurry to go anywhere else.

After all, who would want to give up sunny days and tropical nights for anything else?

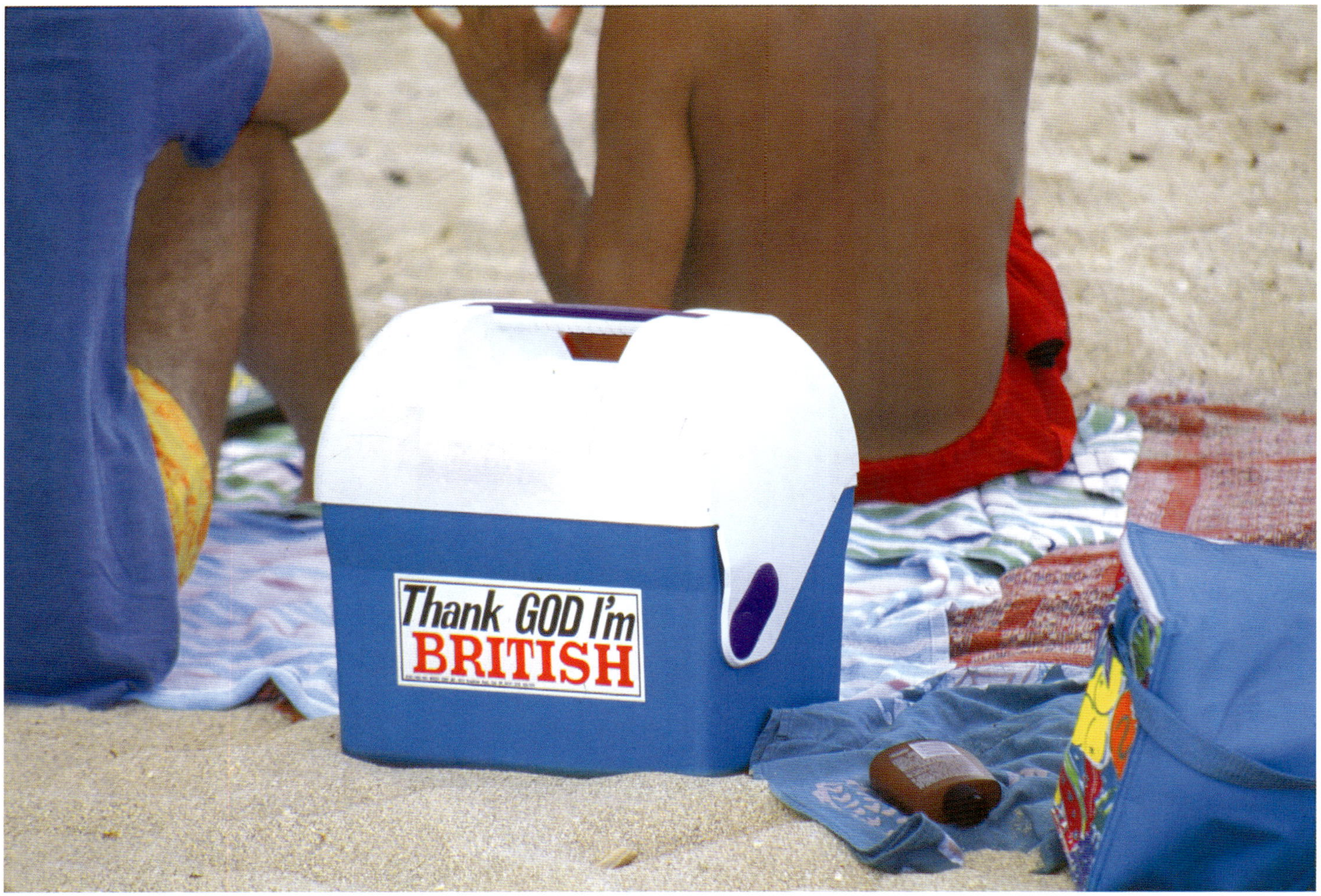

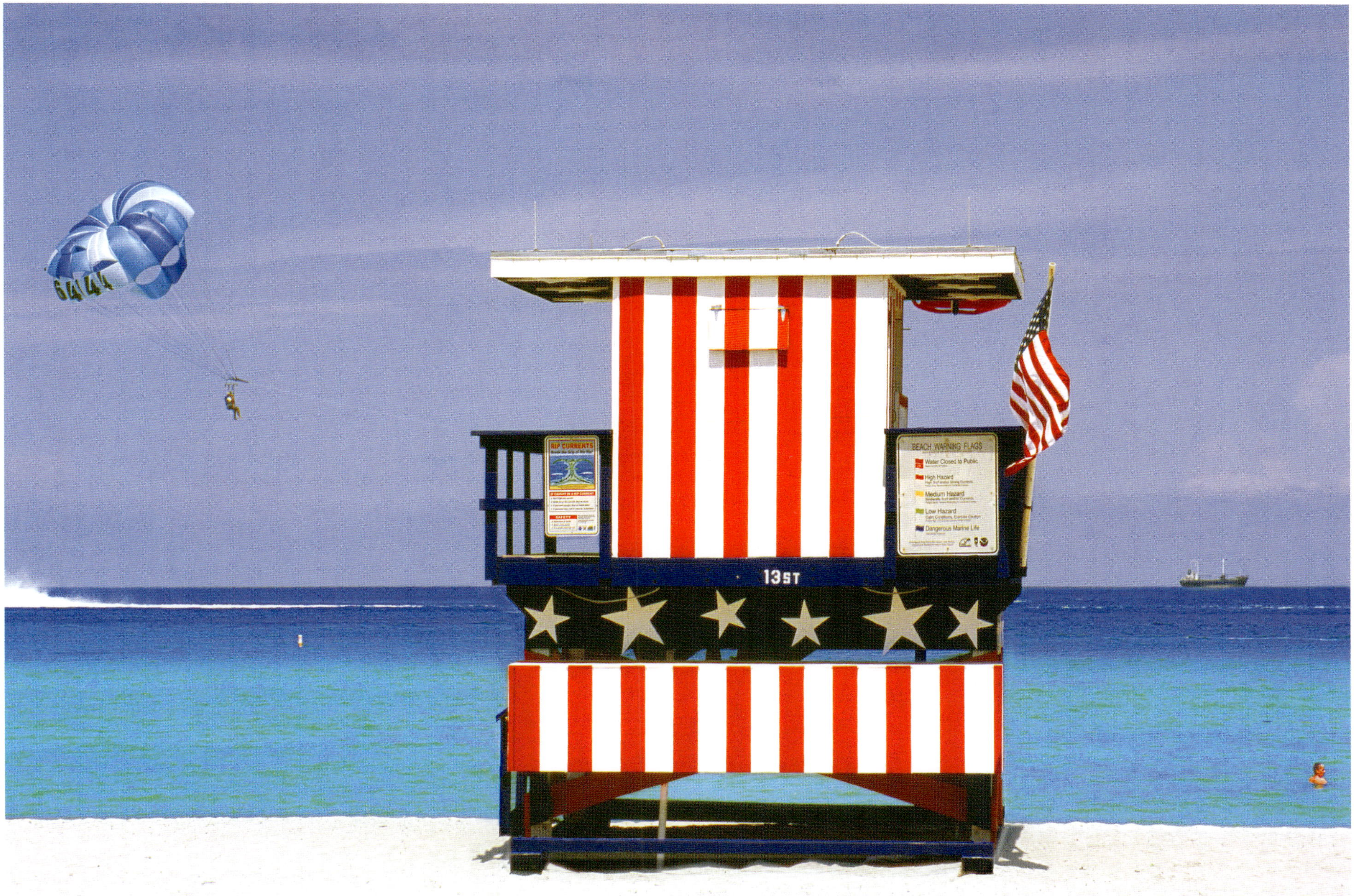
RIP CURRENTS
BEACH WARNING FLAGS
Water Closed to Public
High Hazard
Medium Hazard
Low Hazard
Dangerous Marine Life
13ST

Old 14ST Guardhouse

Golf and the beach are not usually used in the same sentence, especially on South Beach, but here, this little guardhouse – that was created after Hurricane Andrew – sports a faux putting green for a roof. Thus, it was known to some as the "Putting Green Guardhouse," and it stood for years at the 14th Street location, with its funny architecture and bright green and orange colors.

On the June day this picture was taken, everything one could ask for presented itself to the lens.

A live-aboard sailboat passes by, people sun themselves on the beach or cool off in the waters, and a bicyclist talks on his cell phone before heading for a dip into the sea.

Because the guardhouse sits lower than ideal for a good lifeguard view, it was decided to replace it. However, the whimsical lifeguard stand is being saved as an icon and may be on display at the Miami Beach Convention Center, along with one of its cousin stands.

In the companion view taken on another day, the sea is a little "surfy," but evidently very inviting, judging by the number of people in the water. A parasail completes the scene.

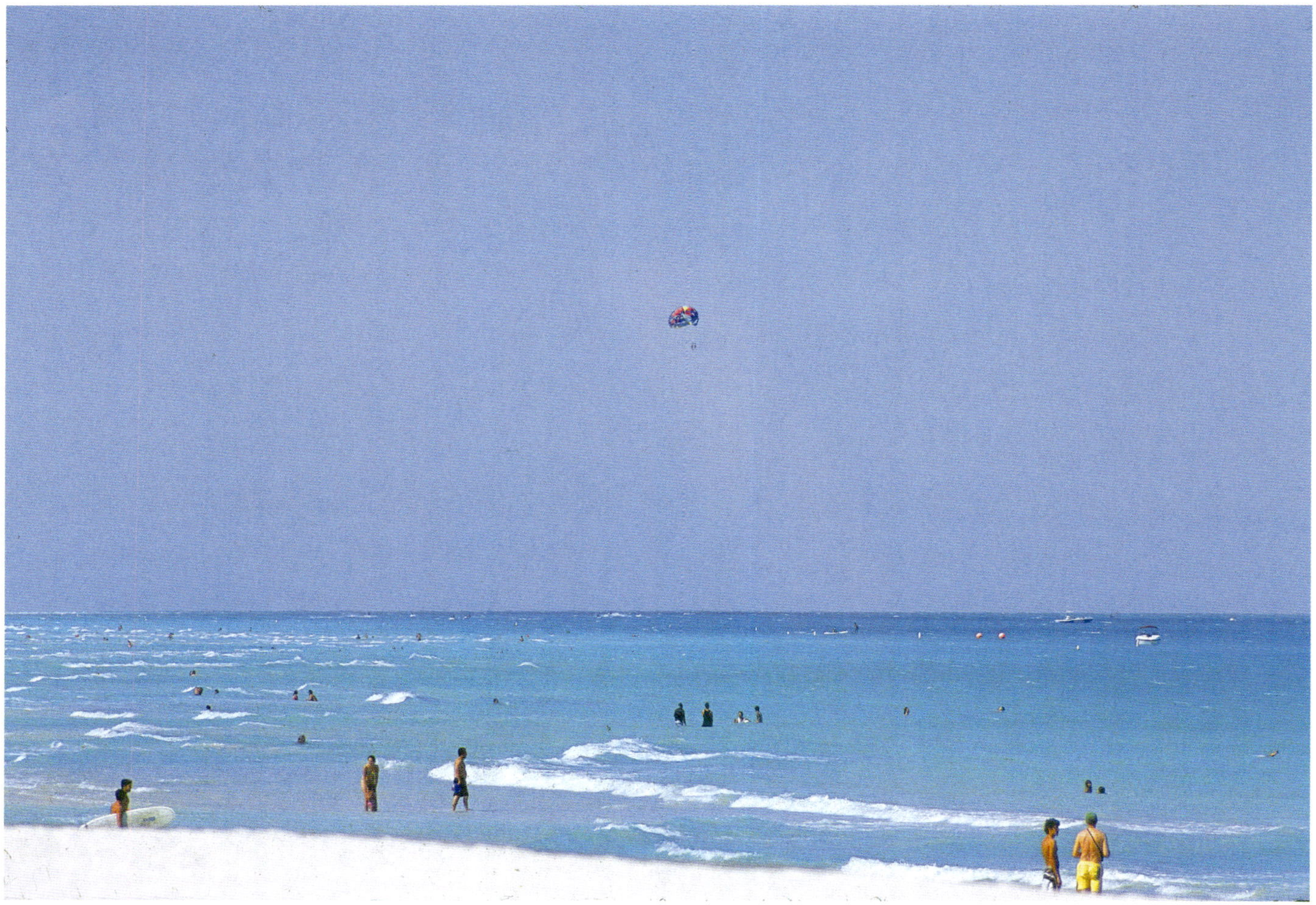

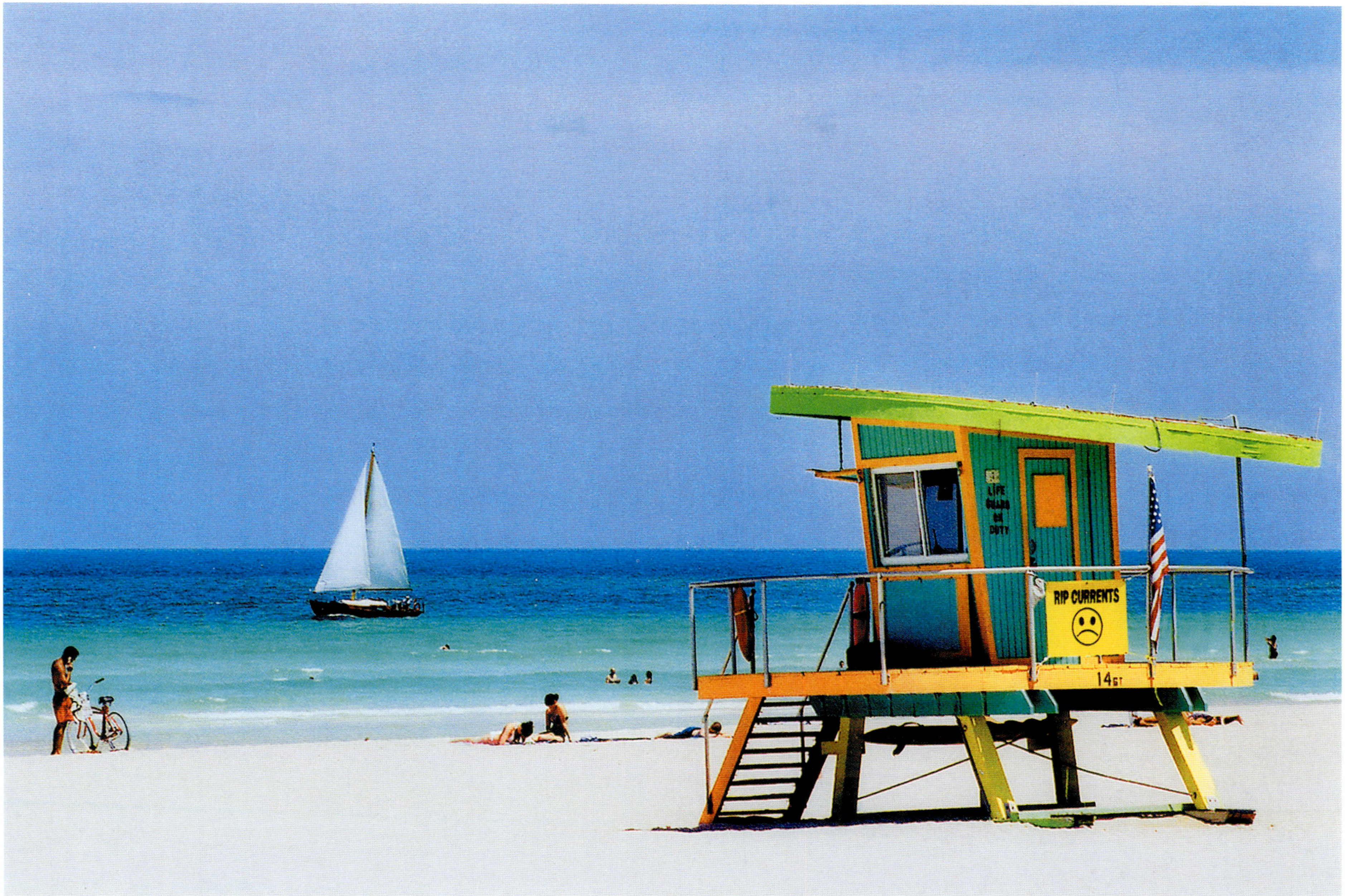
LIFE
GUARD
ON
DUTY
RIP CURRENTS
14 ST

14ST Guardhouse

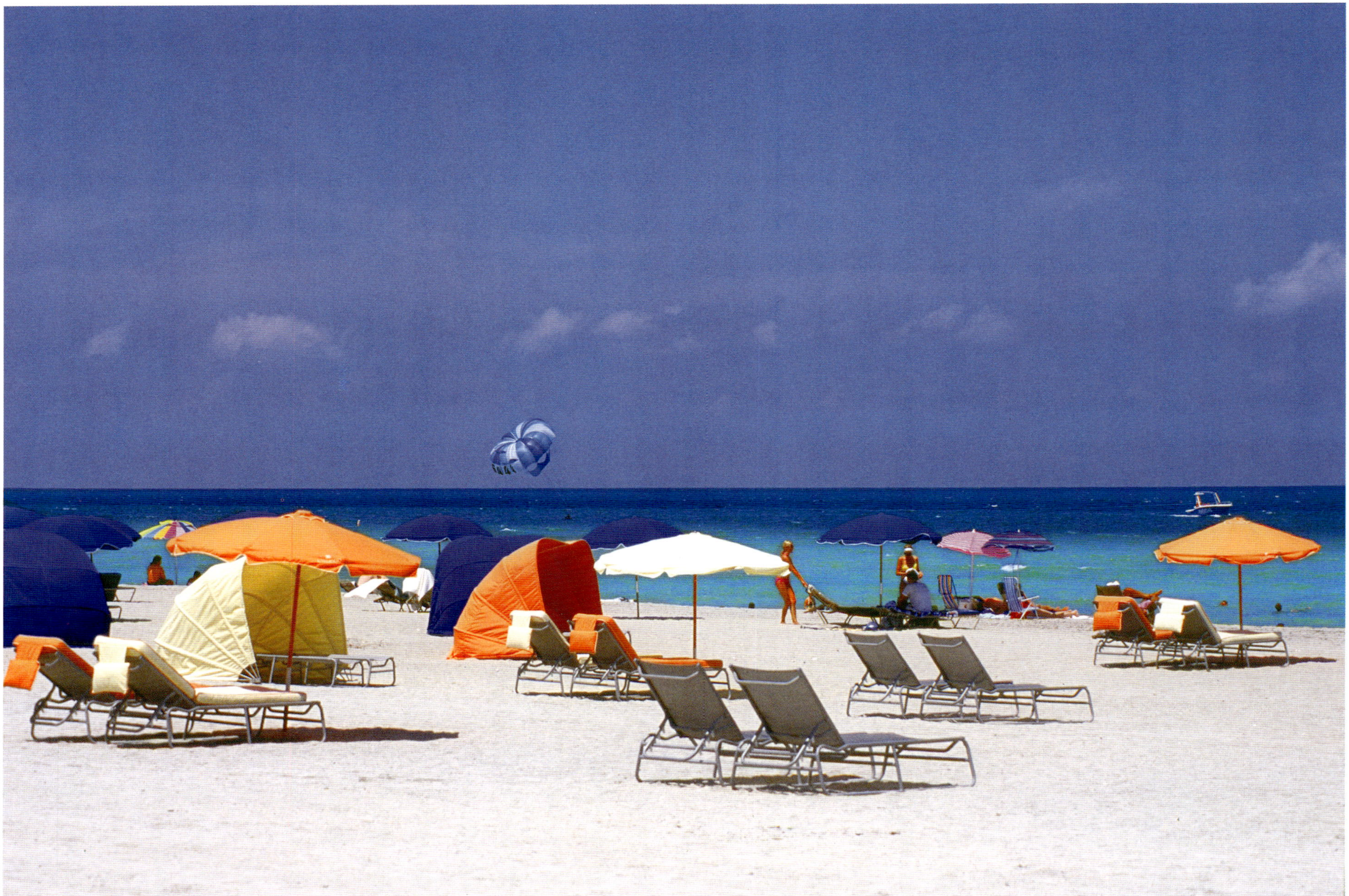

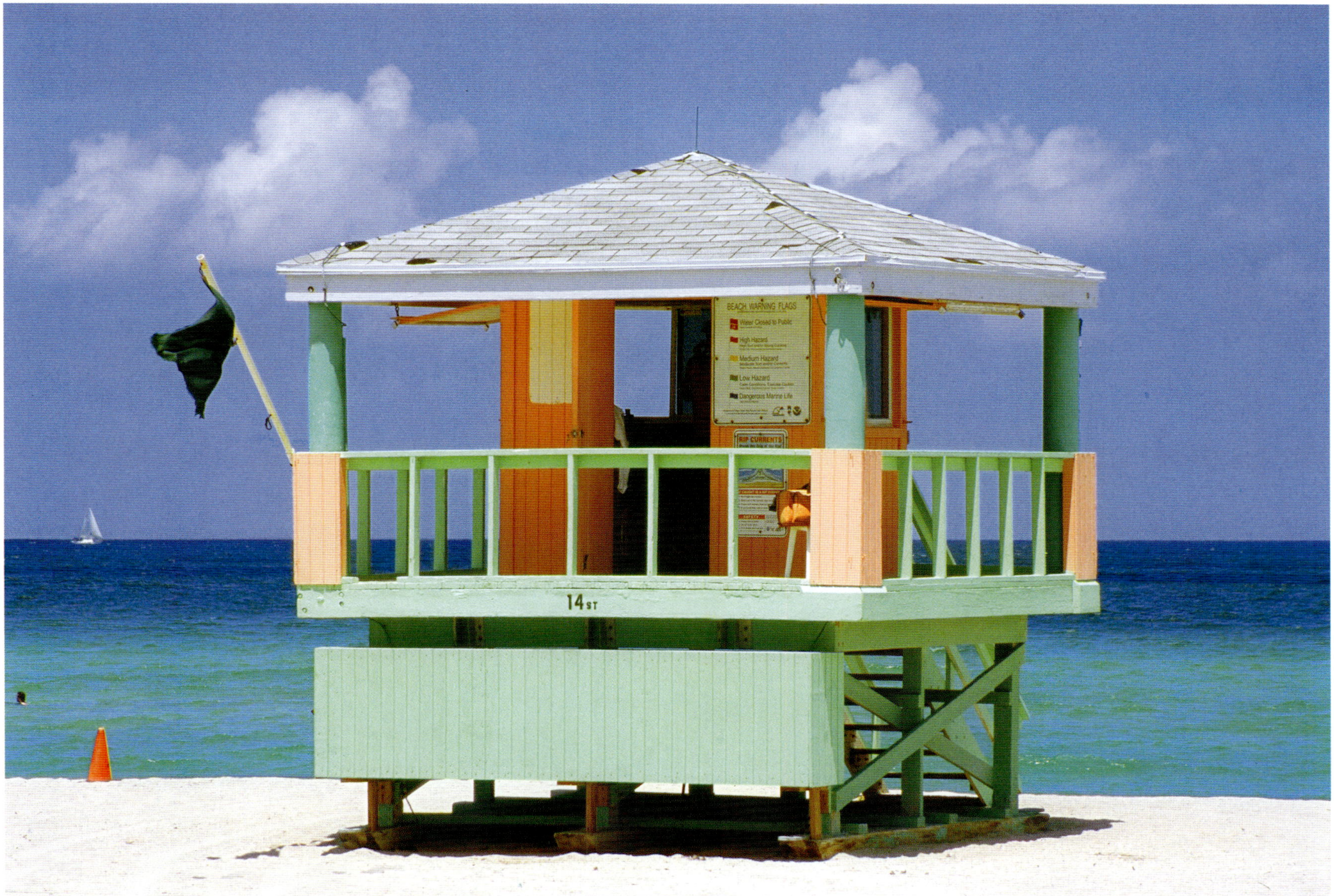

This guardhouse and nearby beach scene were too inviting to resist. A carnival of colors splashes on the panorama, as the one – the lifeguard station – makes one imagine a tiny perfect, beach house, and the other – umbrellas, little cabanas, beach chairs, and a parasail – creates the look of all the fun one can have at the South Beach seashore.

The lifeguard station has its own wraparound balcony, setting off the two-toned light greens that combine with peach and orange, to match up with the sometimes pinkish sands and aqua-green of the sea.

Different from all the other guardhouses, this one began as a kiosk and when it was donated for beach use, a base was added along with the little inside "house," and, voila!, what is now the new 14th Street stand was created.

Just enough clouds in the sky on this June day set the backdrop for this unique lifeguard station, which also marks the end of Lummus Park, which began on 5th Street.

Fourteenth Street on Ocean Drive has a newly renovated and wheelchair accessible restroom facility.

Old 15ST Guardhouse

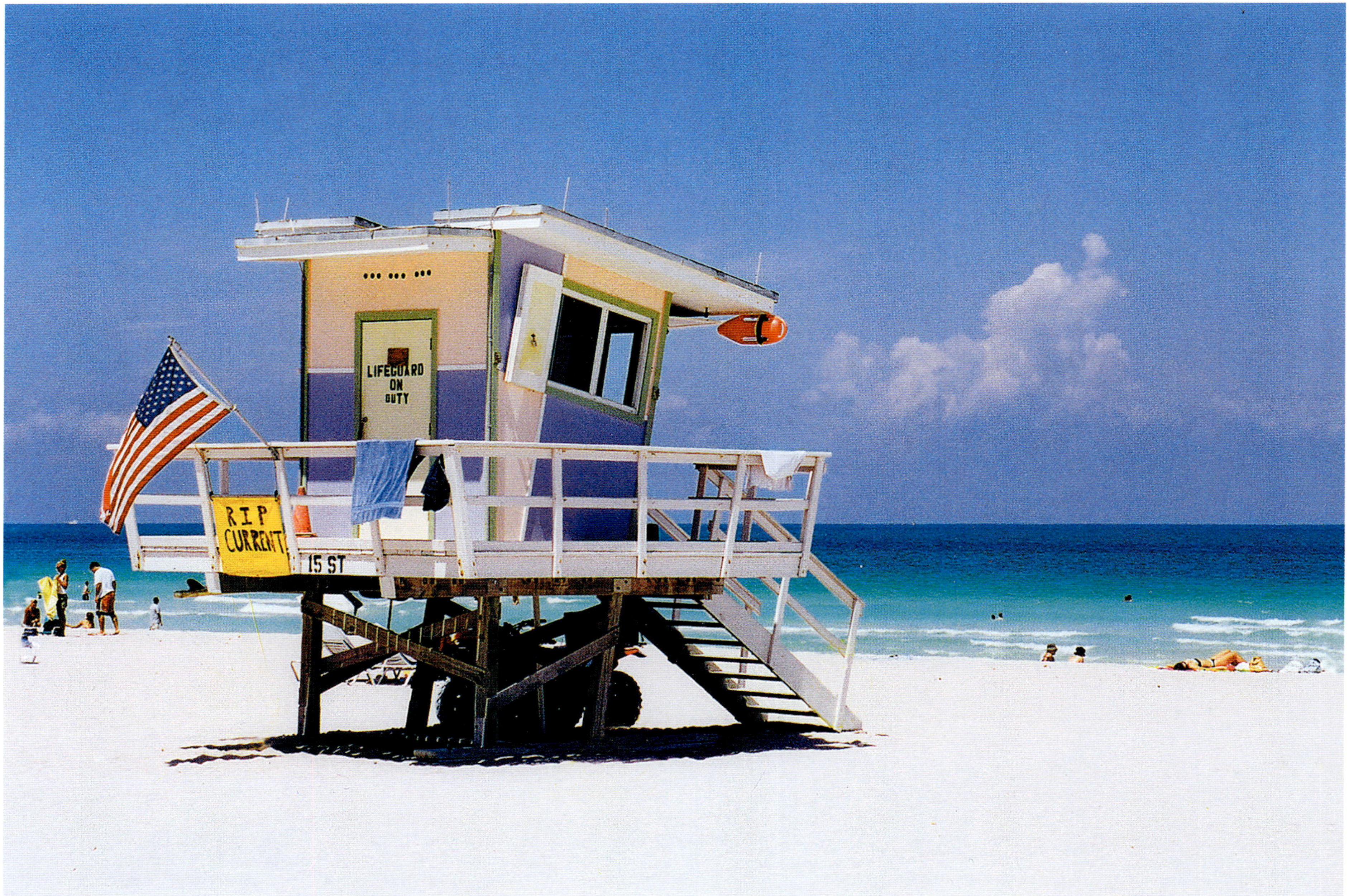

Another of the busiest beach locations on South Beach is at 15th Street, where Lummus Park has ended and some of the biggest hotels and condominiums begin. The cute, little guardhouse that was built after Andrew didn't stand the test of time and later storms, but it was a proud purple and peach-y structure while it lasted. Under the deck is an All-Terrain Vehicle (ATV), used by the lifeguards to travel back to Beach Patrol Headquarters, or to another lifeguard stand in an emergency.

This June day there was an advisory on rip currents, water conditions that can be dangerous to the uninitiated. The currents happen when the wind and the tides work against each other and create areas where a swimmer seemingly cannot swim back to shore. Lifeguards advise anyone caught in one to escape the current rather than try to fight one's way back to shore.

This is done by moving laterally along the shoreline (rather than to or from the beach) until out of the current, when it will once again be easy to swim to shore. If you feel you can't escape the current, then float or tread water and shout and wave for help. That's what the lifeguards are there for.

And, as an added precaution, even on a calm day, never use a raft as a security blanket in the water. Only a good swimmer should use recreational flotation devices in deep water.

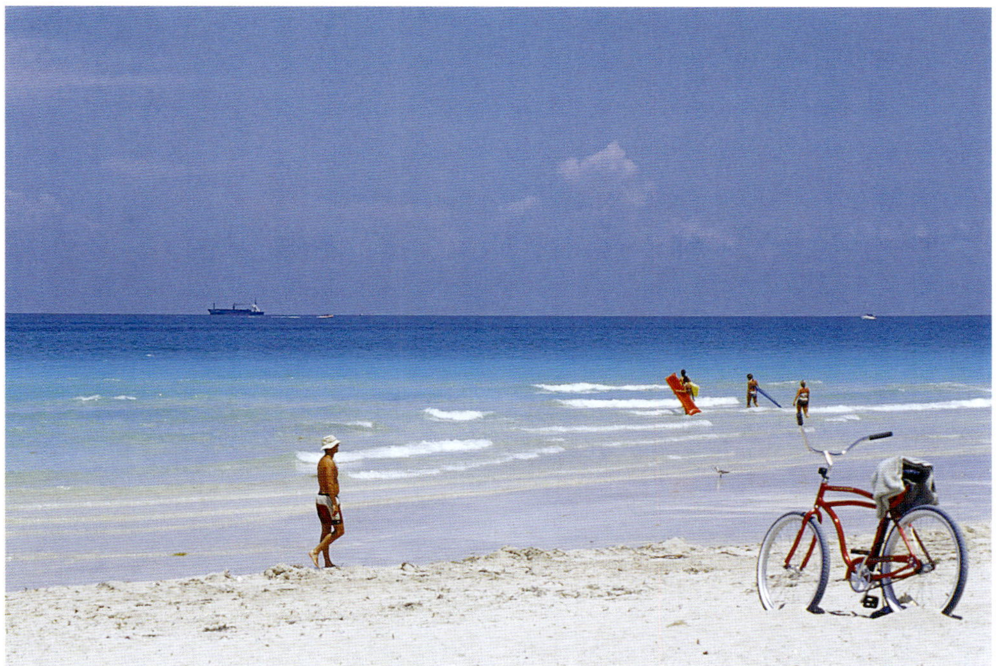

15ST Guardhouse

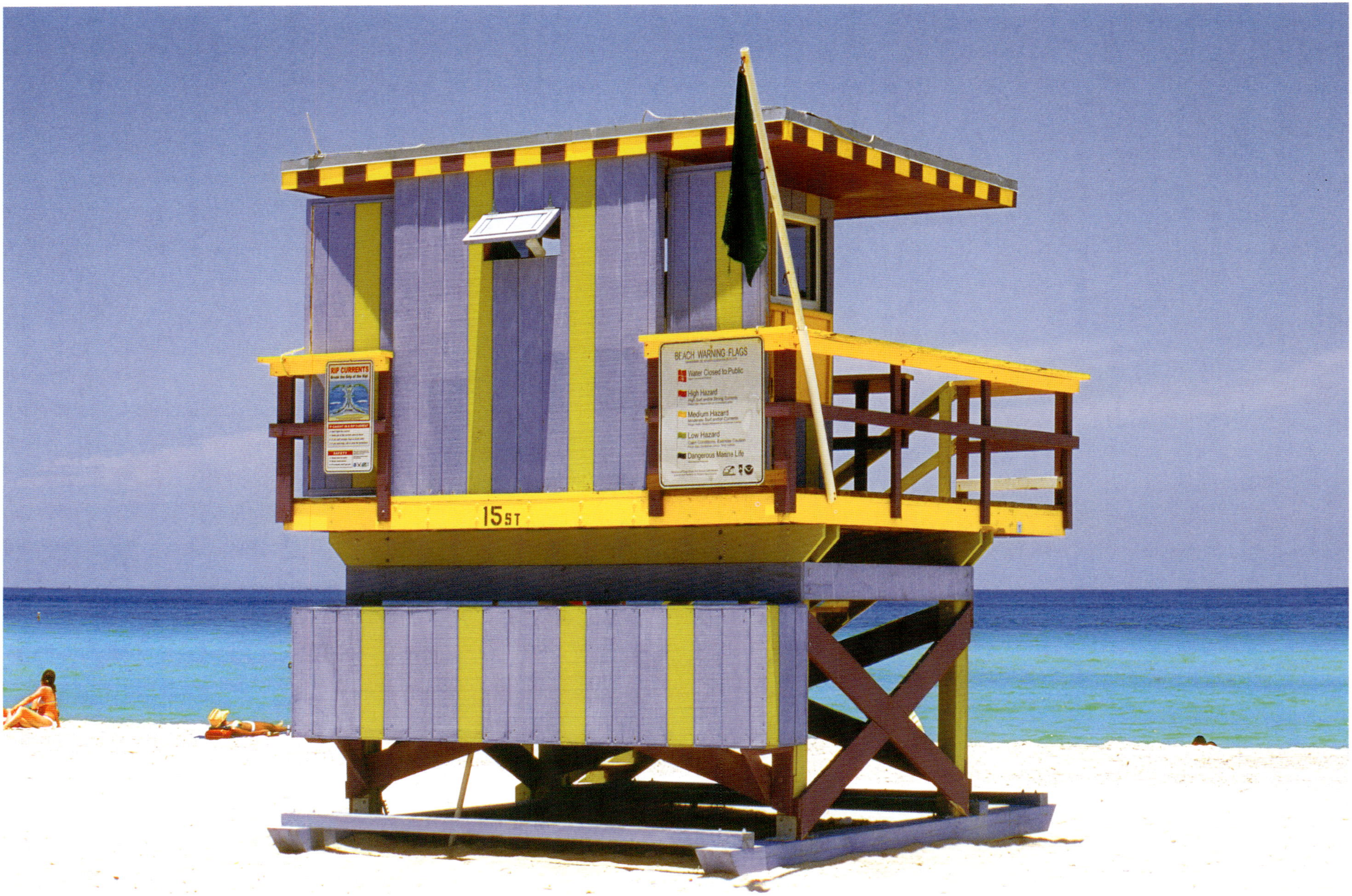

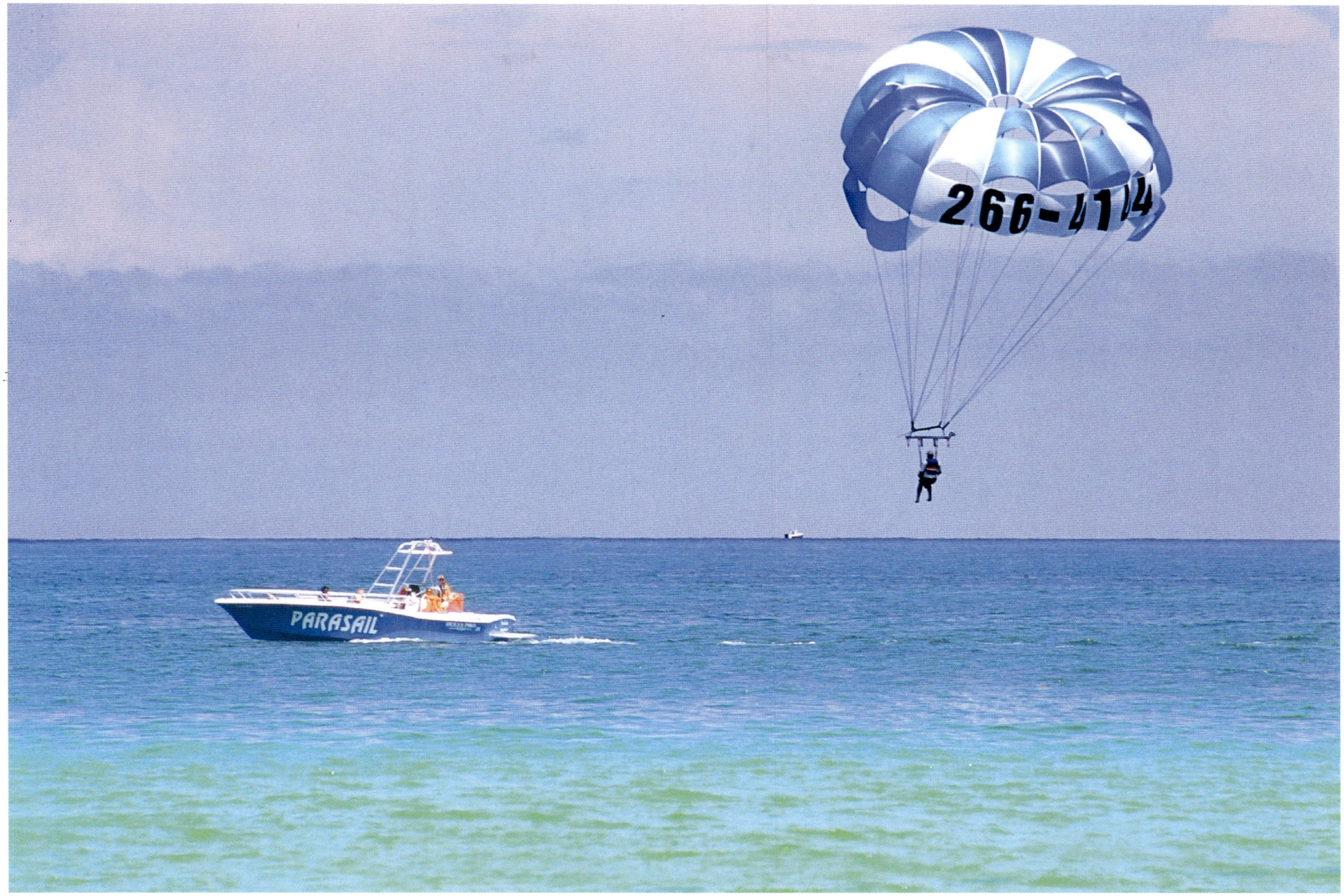

Purple carries on as the main color of the new 15th Street Guardhouse, this one striped in vertical gold. In the event of another strong storm, this lifeguard station, as well as the others, can be hauled to safety on the built-in skids.

Meandering behind this guardhouse and going all the way up to 21st Street is a curving multi-colored brick walkway, sometimes called the Beach Walk. It starts just past 14th Street, where Lummus Park ends, and runs up to the beginning of the wooden boardwalk that covers the beach pathway between 21st and 47th streets. Both at the start and end of the brickway are courtyards of pink, natural, and blue-grey pavers that dramatically illustrate the city's commitment to landscape beauty.

It is at this point -- where the brick path begins at the edge of the park -- that the hotels and condominiums are oceanside, separated from the beach only by the walkway. Ocean Drive has ended here and a jog-in-the-road leads to Collins Avenue.

From the jetty to Fifth Street, the hotels and condos are also oceanside. But along Lummus Park, all structures are on the opposite side of the street, which is Ocean Drive.

Anywhere along the beach and on any calm day like this June afternoon, one is likely to see a parasail aloft over the turquoise waters of the ocean. Lucky parasailors, lucky beachgoers.

16ST Guardhouse

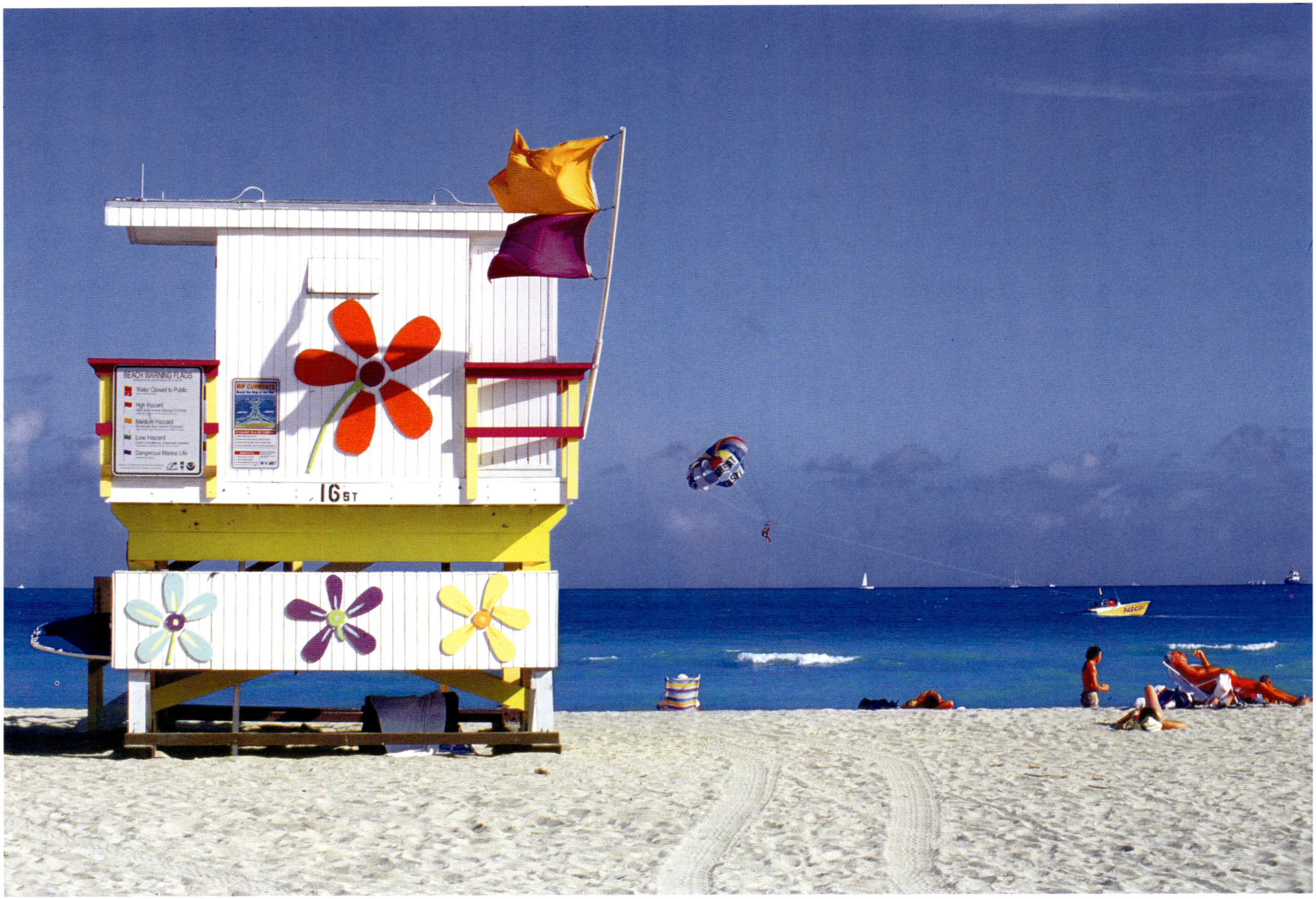

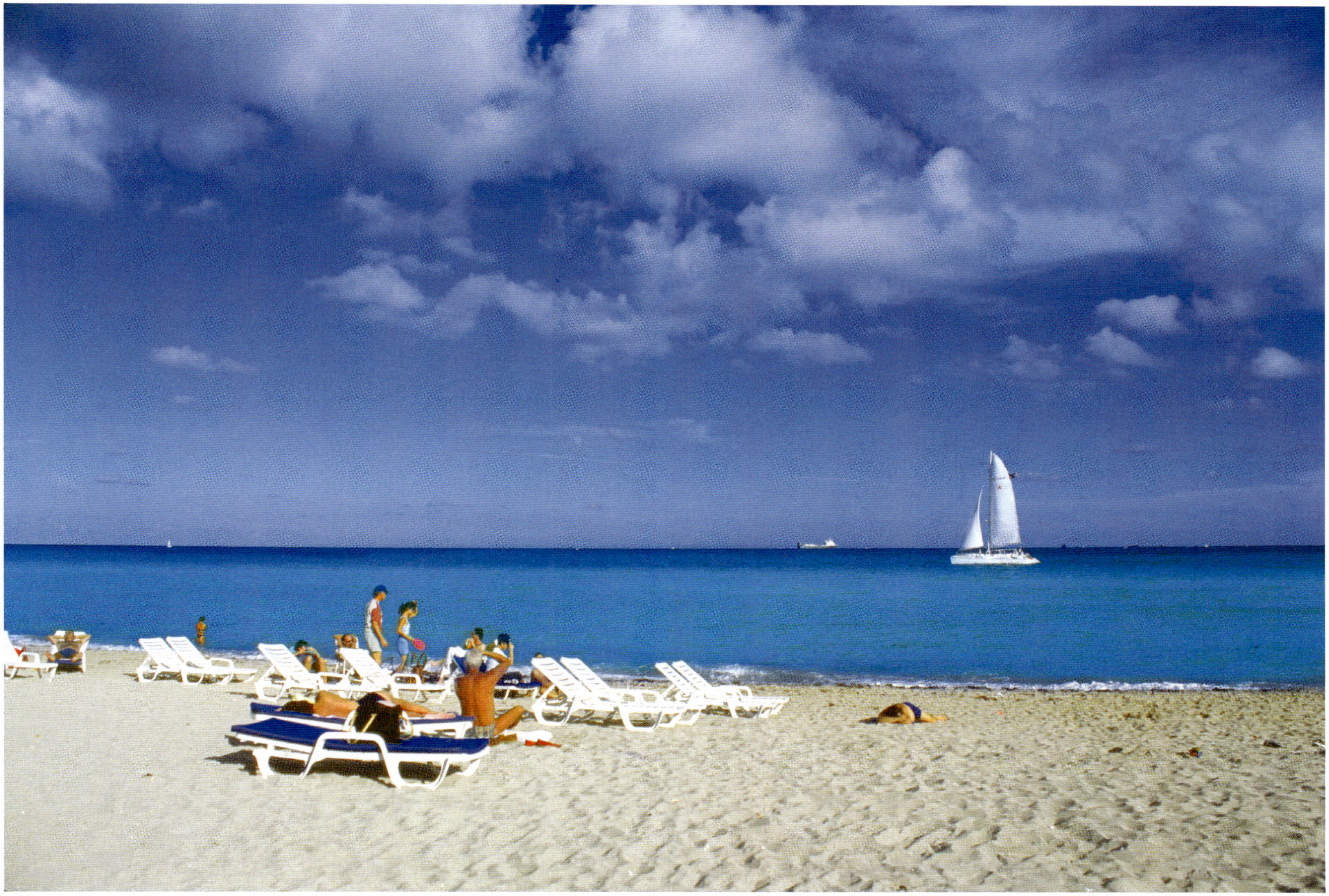

This January day was windy with some water advisories in effect, but the afternoon was too beautiful to keep snowbirds away from the charming 16th Street Guardhouse. There is always the sun to enjoy, the tan to get (with sunscreen, hopefully), and a parasail to ride if the wind isn't too strong.

A windy day like this is a water sailor's delight, too, and on this one and most others, sailboats grace the horizon off Miami Beach as they glide and bob along in a silent seagoing world of adventure and delight.

Sometimes called the "Flower Guardhouse," the 16th Street lifeguard station is meticulously decorated with bursts of colorful blooms, not all parts of which stay on the guardhouse from month to month. Misguided souvenir hunters sometimes pry off pieces of the flowers, ruining the effect and forcing the city to recut, repaint, and replace the lost sections. So much better to respect the talent and skill that went into the decorating, and leave all the parts in place.

The 16th Street Guardhouse is in the vicinity of some of the city's largest hotels, and many of them provide rentable beach chairs and umbrellas, as well as children's play areas.

Old 17ST Guardhouse

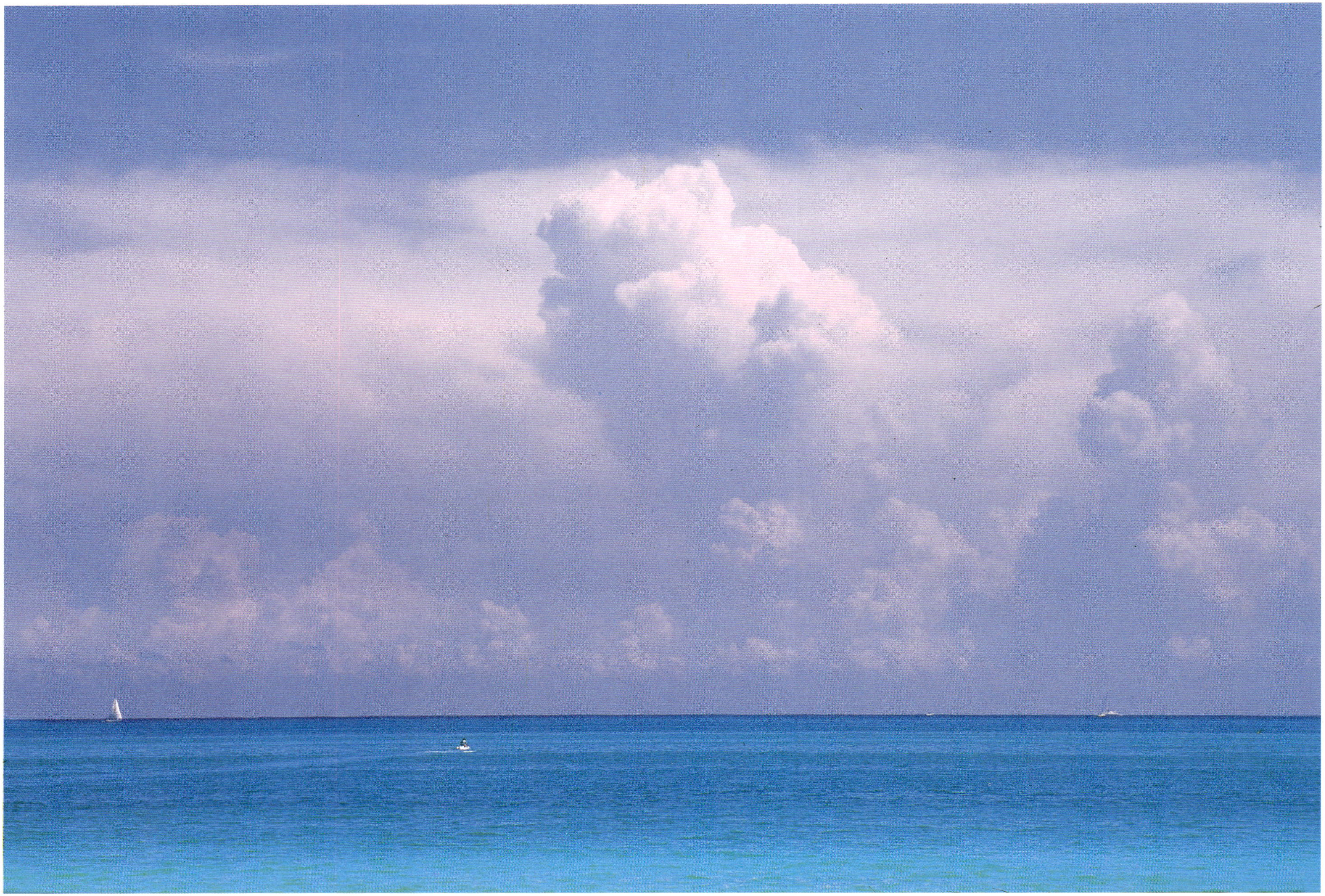

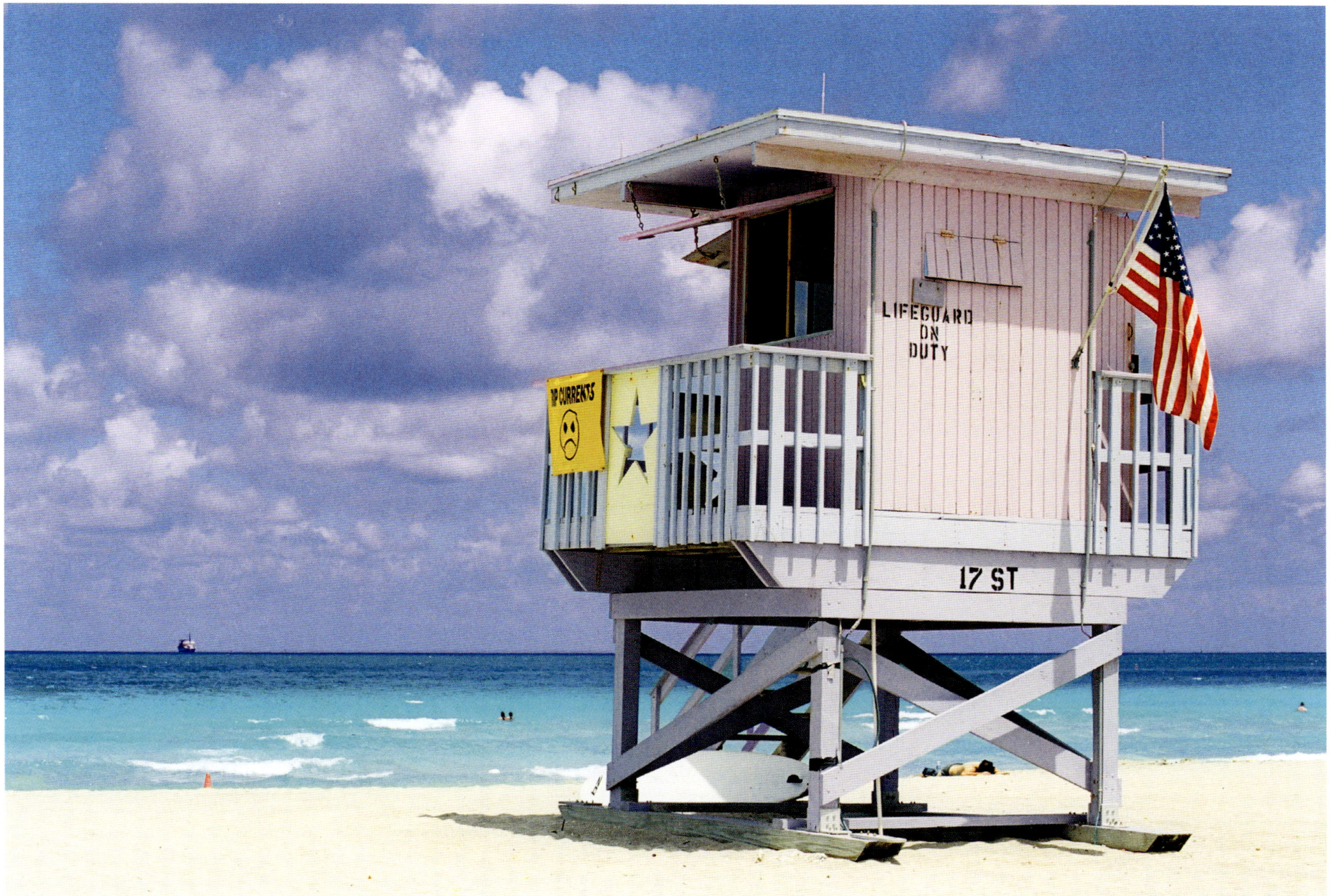

Pretty in pink, the 17th Street Guardhouse didn't make it through one of the major storms in the fall of 2005. It had all the desirable prerequisites for permanence – it stood high enough off the sand for a good lifeguard view, had pull-away skids in case of a big storm, and it perfectly matched the massive pinkish clouds that sometimes cover the skies off Miami Beach. But, alas, it was not to be, and it remains as a sweet memory.

The rip current signs seen here with the non-smiley face are no longer in use, and color flags now fly on all the guardhouses to notify swimmers of water conditions.

Turquoise waters that look good enough to float on, swim in, and dive under, contrast the South Beach skies that range from the pink shades here to crimson and orange, yellows and purples, even black and blue.

It's no wonder that models and directors and writers have chosen this South Florida wonderland as a setting for their glossy ads, flashy high-speed movie chases, and glitzy storytelling.

There is no shortage here of the "*je ne sais quoi*" needed for any media event, whatever the dimensions, wherever the locale, whoever the celebrity. After all, this is South Beach!

17ST Guardhouse

This one's by the children and for the children! Adorable wouldn't adequately describe the new 17th Street Guardhouse, which is covered in ceramic sea life crafted by Miami Beach schoolchildren at a city recreation center.

Fish and seahorses and little water scenes were shaped and brilliantly painted by these kids for this particular purpose, and what a worthy project it was. They created something very special and the lifeguard station is receiving a lot of well-deserved attention.

Adjacent to the "Ceramic Guardhouse" is a play area set up by a nearby hotel that continues with a children's theme. A pristine rowboat under white umbrellas sits on the sand, surrounded by colorful little buckets and shovels. Made for climbing on and digging in, kids can have fun while their parents relax on a chaise lounge, keeping a watchful eye, of course.

South Beach shows again and again, it is as much for families as it is for singles and young couples, as much for sailing enthusiasts as swimmers, as much for the big-hatted, buttoned-up, stay in the shade at all costs visitor as it is for the sun-seeker.

In South Beach, there is something for everyone.

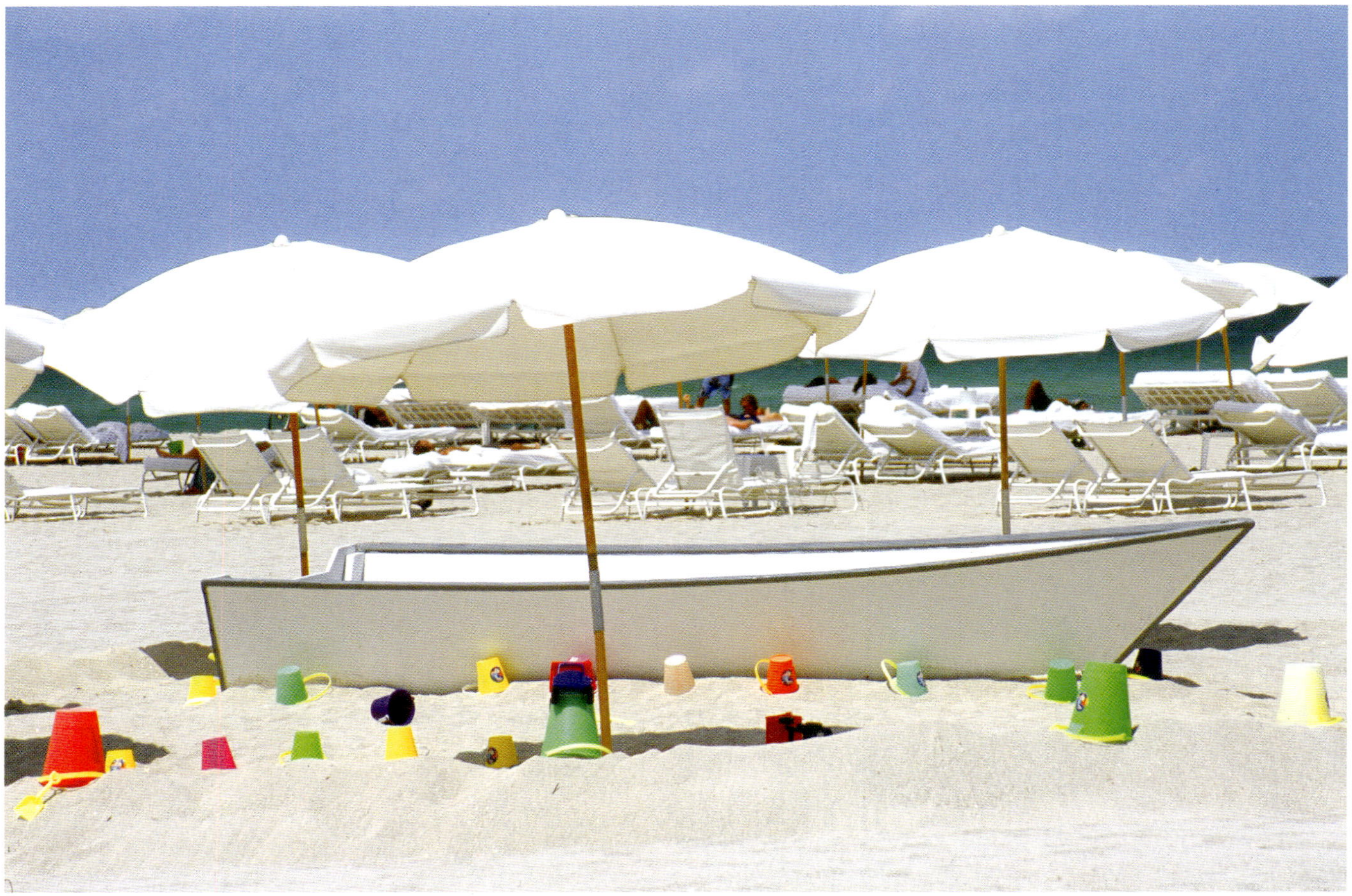

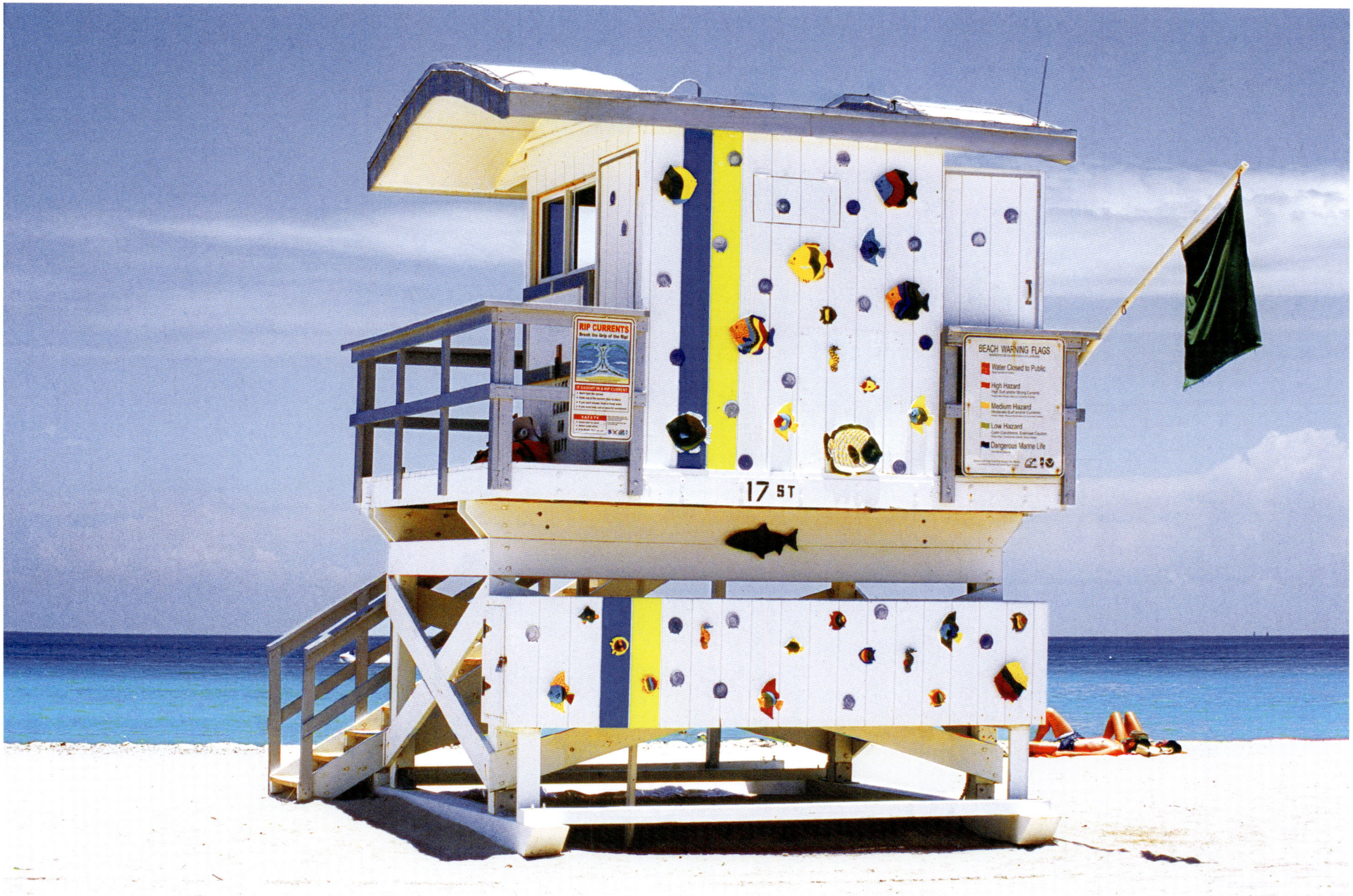
RIP CURRENTS
Break the Grip of the Rip!
IF CAUGHT IN A RIP CURRENT
SAFETY
17 ST
BEACH WARNING FLAGS
Water Closed to Public
High Hazard
High Surf and/or Strong Currents
Medium Hazard
Moderate Surf and/or Currents
Low Hazard
Calm Conditions, Exercise Caution
Dangerous Marine Life

35ST Guardhouse

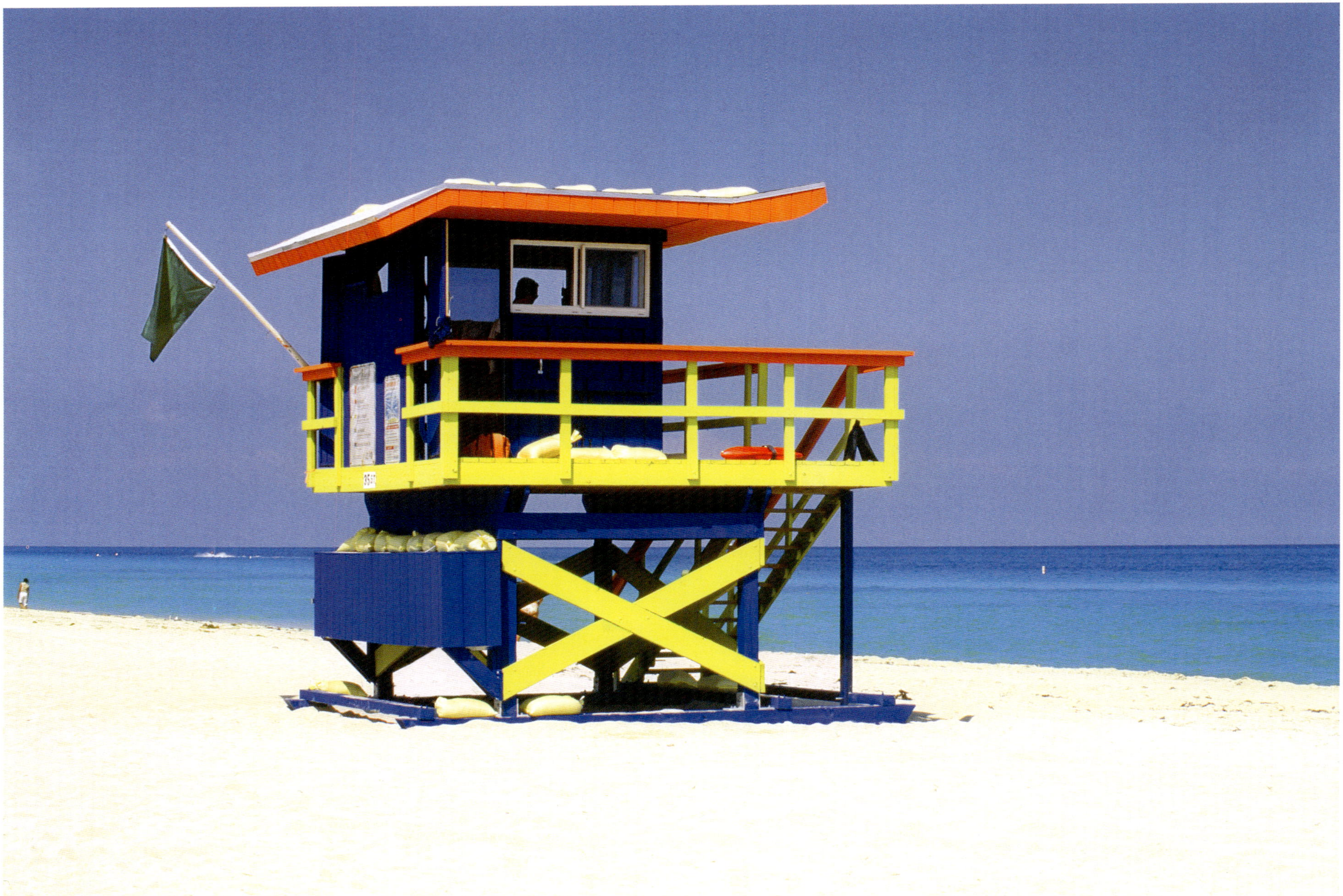

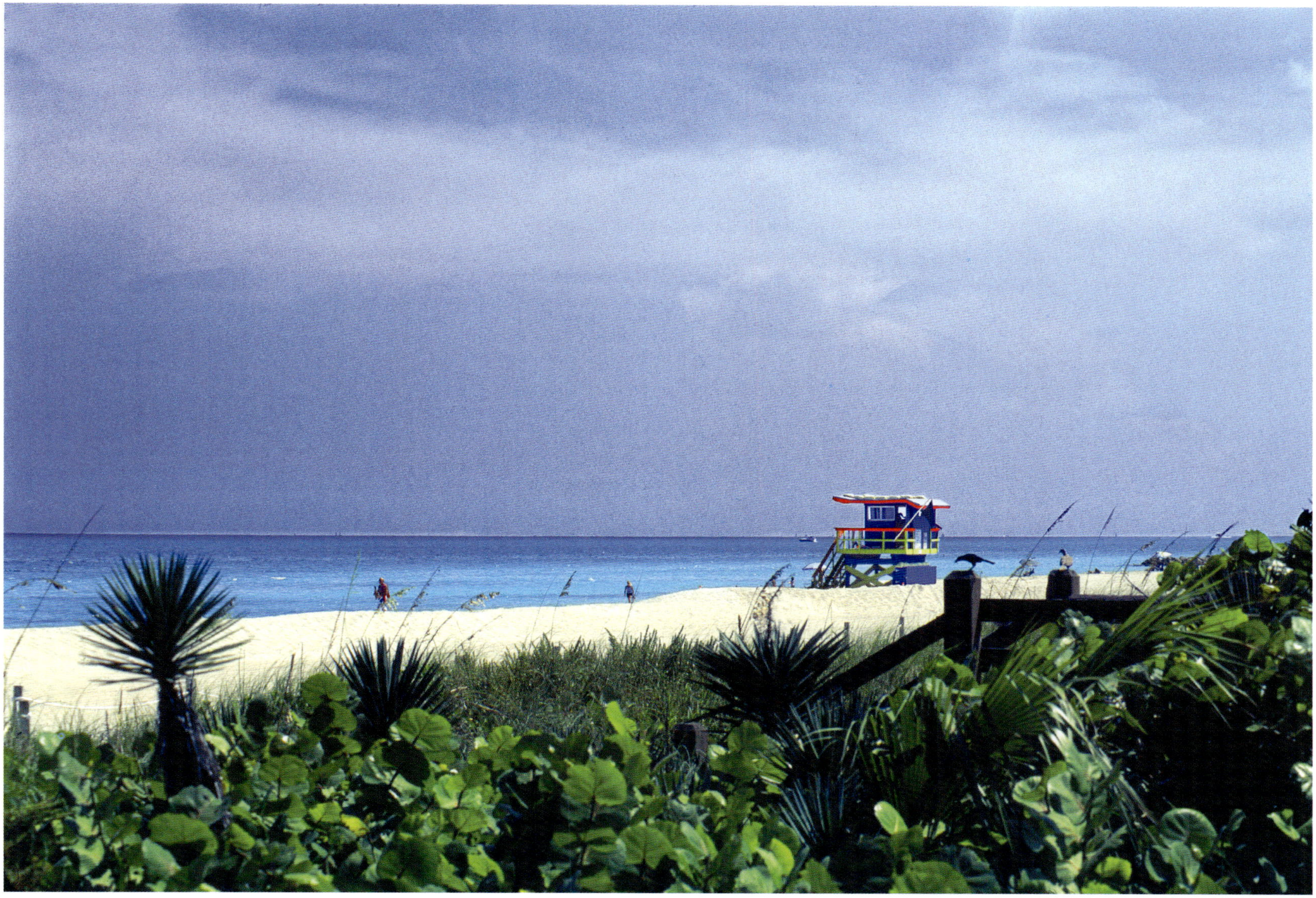

On a September day, deep purple characterizes this sturdy guardhouse on 35th Street, a color which is set off by its bright red/orange and yellow trim. It is one of the guardhouses backed by a wonderful, wide, wooden boardwalk that has amenities beyond those of a simple walkway.

Beginning at 21st Street and ending at 47th, the boardwalk provides an excellent passageway for visitors on foot only – runners, walkers, sightseers, and beachgoers. Throughout the length of it are rest areas that provide benches and plenty of shade under tiled roofs. Some of these oases have emergency call buttons, all of them have lots of room.

From the boardwalk, there is a superb view of the ocean and ships on the horizon. Because these more northern beaches are often less crowded than the ones on South Beach, the view is also more unencumbered up and down the shoreline and this carnival-colored guardhouse can be seen from a great distance.

The boardwalk is also a good place to study the sand dunes from its raised perspective. Sand dunes everywhere on the beaches are strictly off limits for walking through, or plucking any vegetation, and their contents can be hard to see at ground level. Here on the boardwalk, there is a good view down into the dune.

46ST Guardhouse

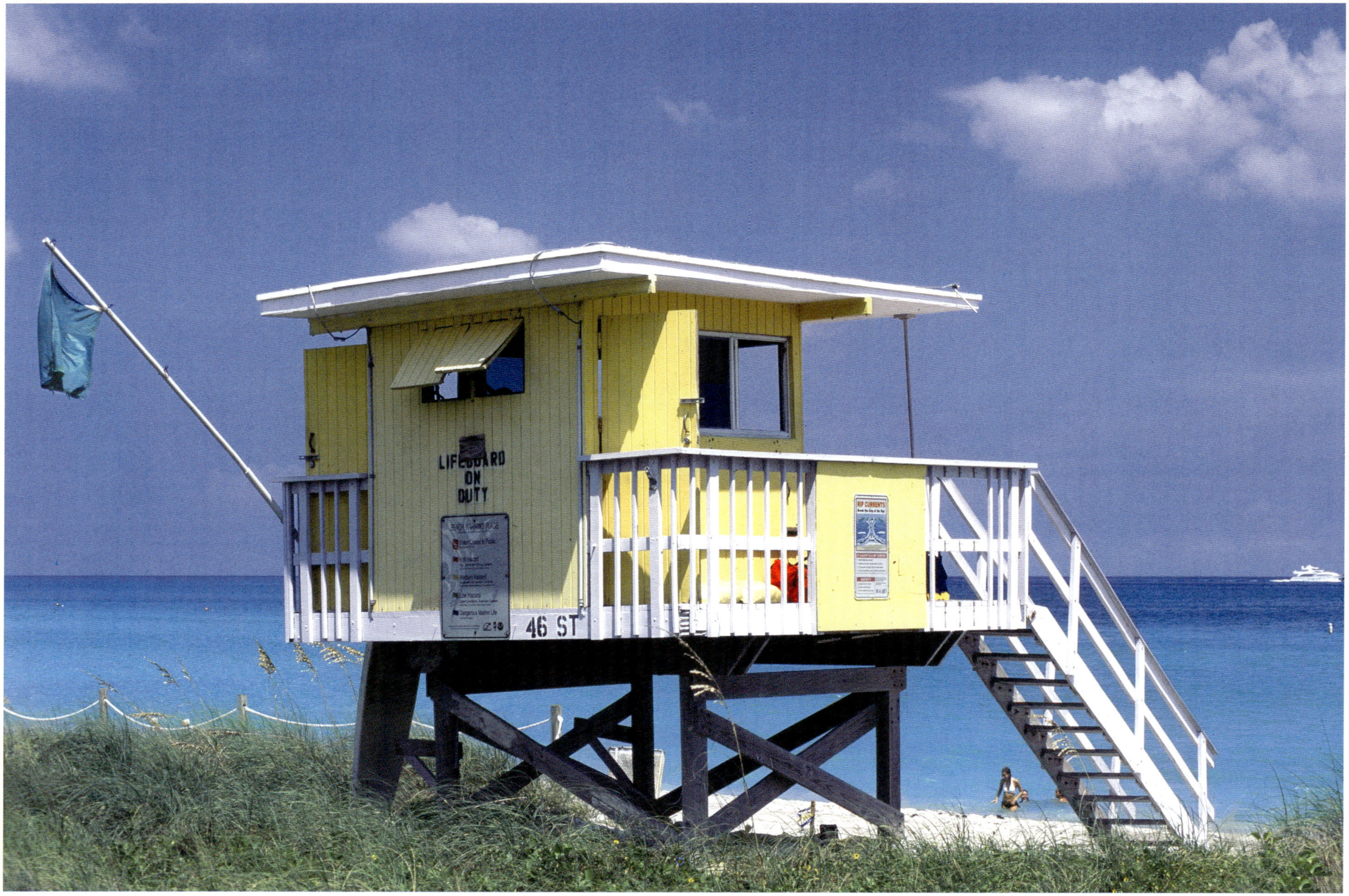

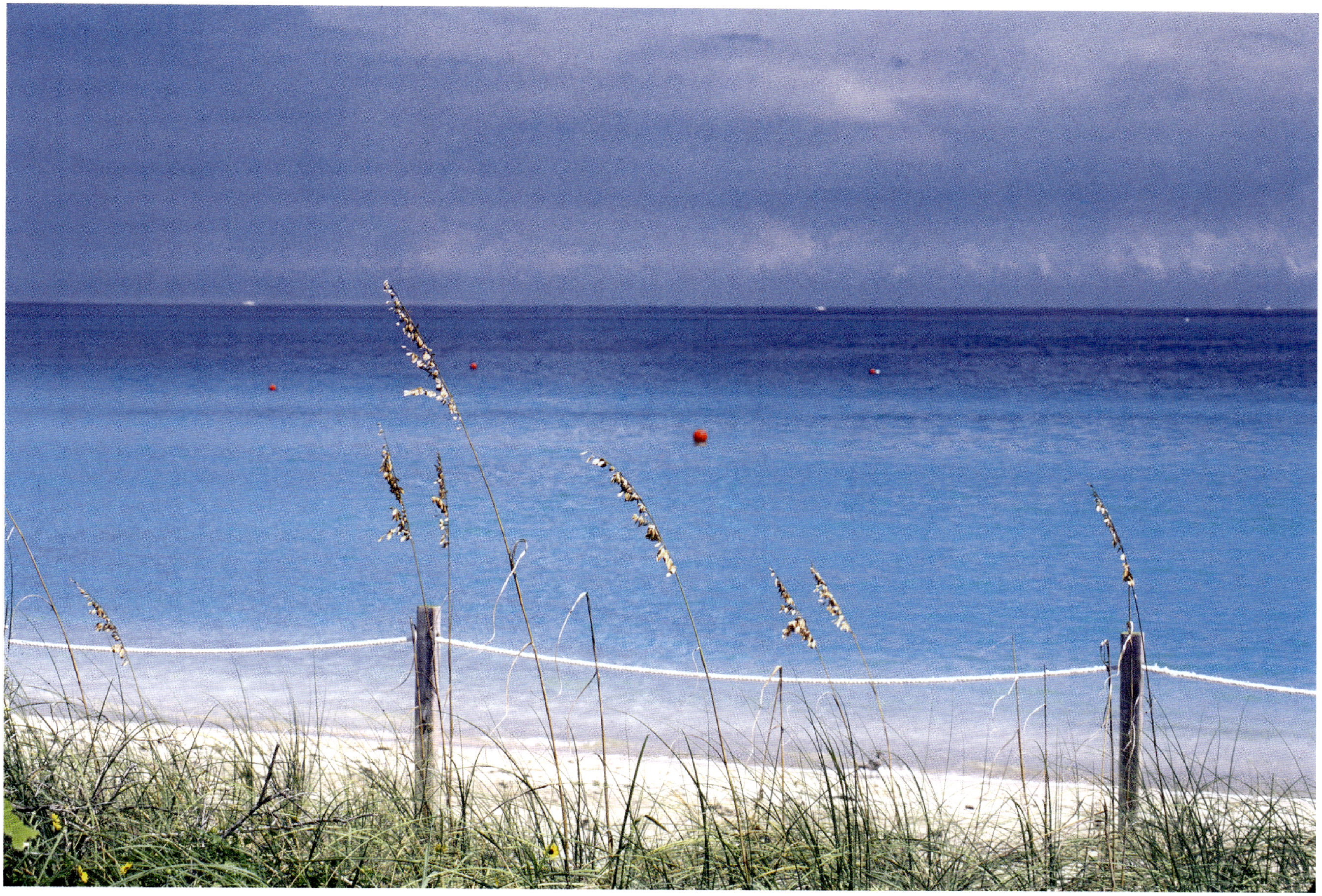

Driving up Collins Avenue, the roadway takes a curving jog beyond 43rd Street onto the famous route that is known here as AIA, as well as Collins. Perched between the Intracoastal Waterway and the Atlantic, the visitor has arrived in a very interesting area with classic mansions clearly visible across the waterway to the left and famous hotels along Collins on the right.

Also, very shortly on the right will be the entrance to the public parking lot at the 46th Street Guardhouse. There is space for hundreds of cars, with the added bonus of a pay telephone, drinking fountains, and bath and changing rooms with wheelchair access.

The elevated wooden boardwalk ends at this sometimes less busy and bright yellow guardhouse, and it is a great spot for sea-gazing and getting a good look at the endangered sea oats. One might even get poetic here, on this September day, a la John Masefield: "...I must down to the seas again, to the lonely sea and the sky..."

Well, perhaps not really lonely. Remember that parking lot with hundreds of spaces?

74ST Guardhouse

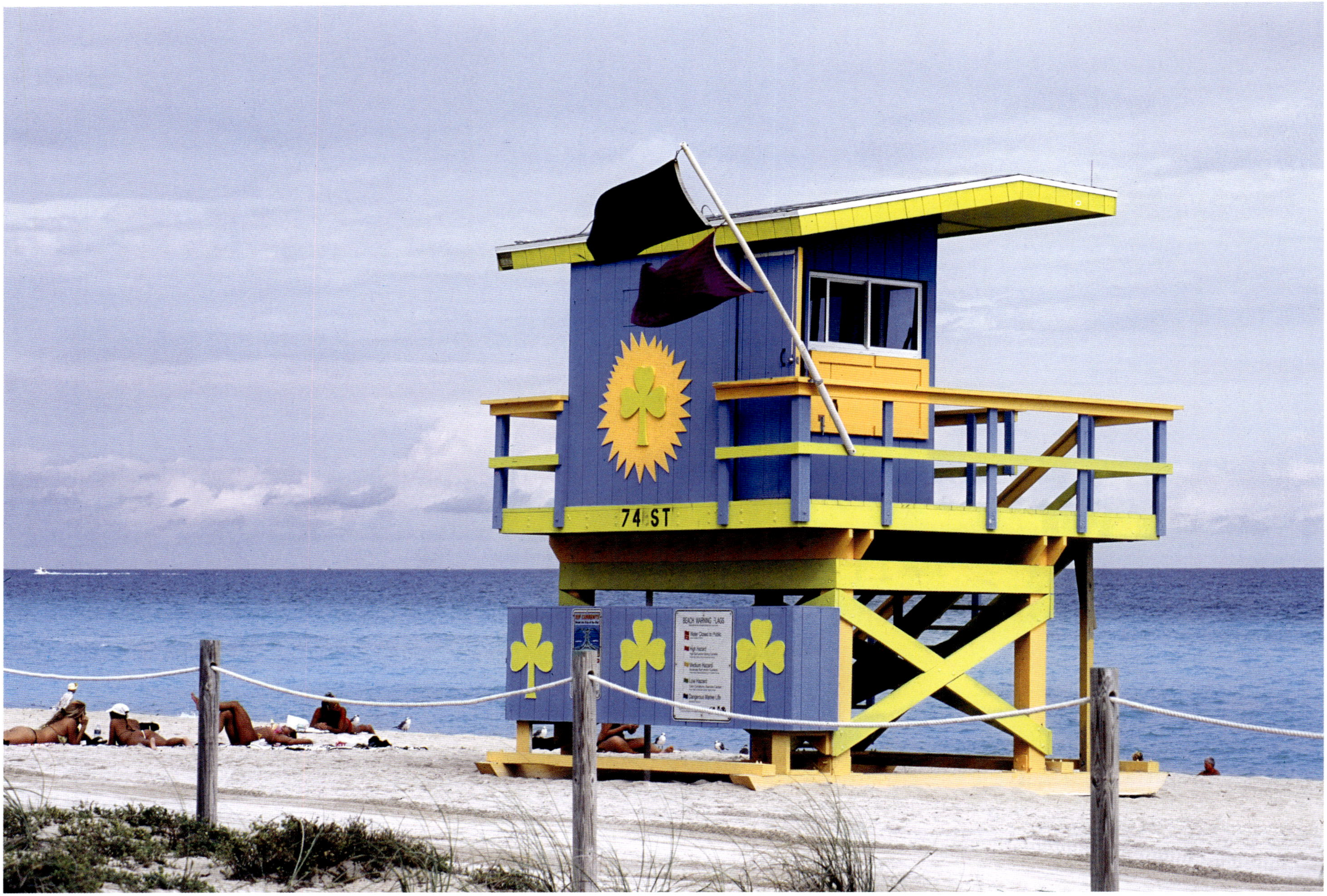

A golden sunburst and bright shamrocks celebrate this Irish-themed guardhouse on 74th Street. Somewhere between deep lavender and purple, the guardhouse color is offset by the attached shamrocks that are somewhere between yellow and chartreuse. Not quite this and not quite that. Visitors love the distinctive guardhouse, which is set off a street that must be the best kept secret in Miami Beach.

Called Ocean Terrace, it can be accessed on 73rd, 74th, or 75th streets. The terrace is a three-block short street of brick sidewalks, graceful palm trees, and easy parking. The ocean side is vegetation and beach only, with little Art Deco gem buildings, some not yet renovated, on the opposite side of the street.

This street eventually will be a show-stopper, but even now the visitor can find such delights on it as an authentic outdoor Italian restaurant and hotels just steps from the beach.

And on this January day, as on most days, the sun is bright enough, the temperature warm enough, and the sky blue enough for the beach to be a major attraction.

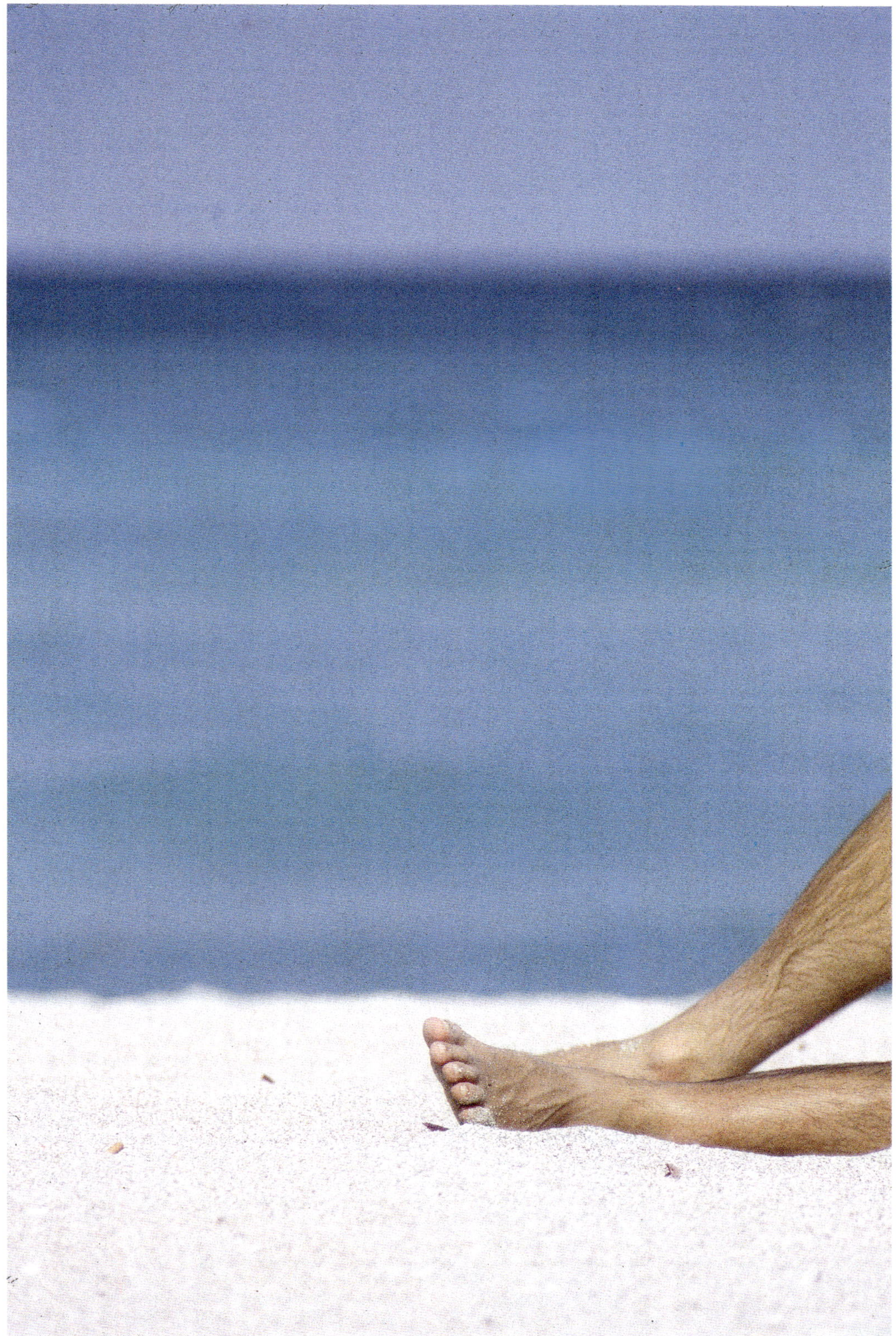

The Way We Were

That was now, and this is then, the way we were in the early 1990s, when these pictures were taken. We were beautiful then but it was yet to be discovered how beautiful. We were preserved, with the Art Deco movement already underway, but many renovations were just beginning (and are still on-going) and what was yet to be uncovered and saved resulted in a remarkable transformation of much of Miami Beach.

What had been an ocean side resort in decline became a butterfly taking wing to inform the world that Miami Beach was back as a first-tier destination, this time a media mecca, this time a star of television, movies, and print, this time a choice locale for celebrities and the ambitious young who came not so much to sit back; but to sit up to take notice and to be noticed; to open restaurants at noon and close clubs at dawn.

Fortunes were made and lost and made again. Some boutiques that opened in the heyday of newness and reasonable rents, lost their leases in the rising cost of square-footage to the national chains. Chefs made names for themselves in a city that was once better known for good delis and early dinner specials.

Miami Beach became another entity from those early days, and if beauty is in the eye of the beholder, it is passing a new test every day because there are visitors from every corner of the earth who make South Beach/Miami Beach their top vacation destination every year. The magnificent ocean and beautiful beach play no small role in that choice.

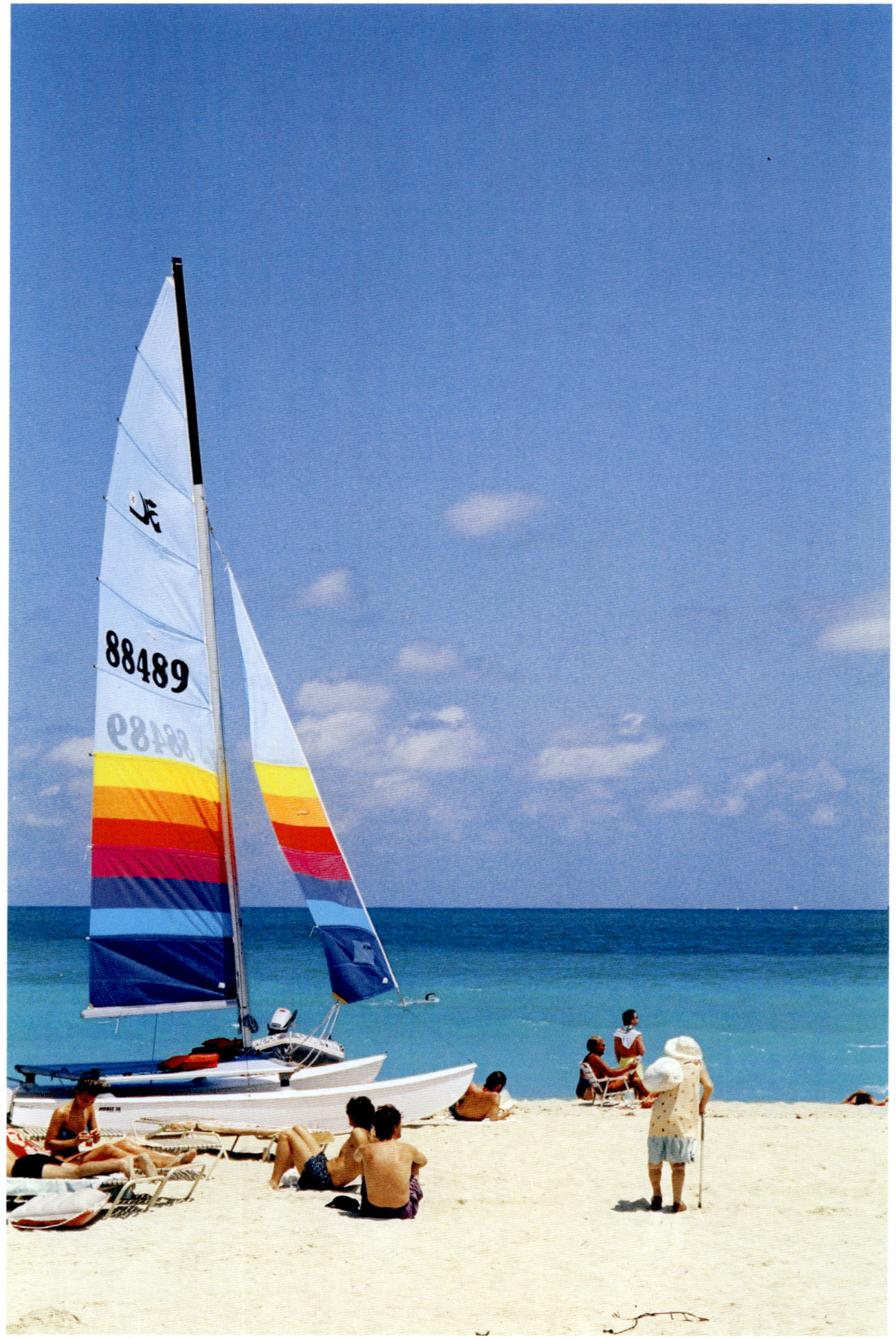

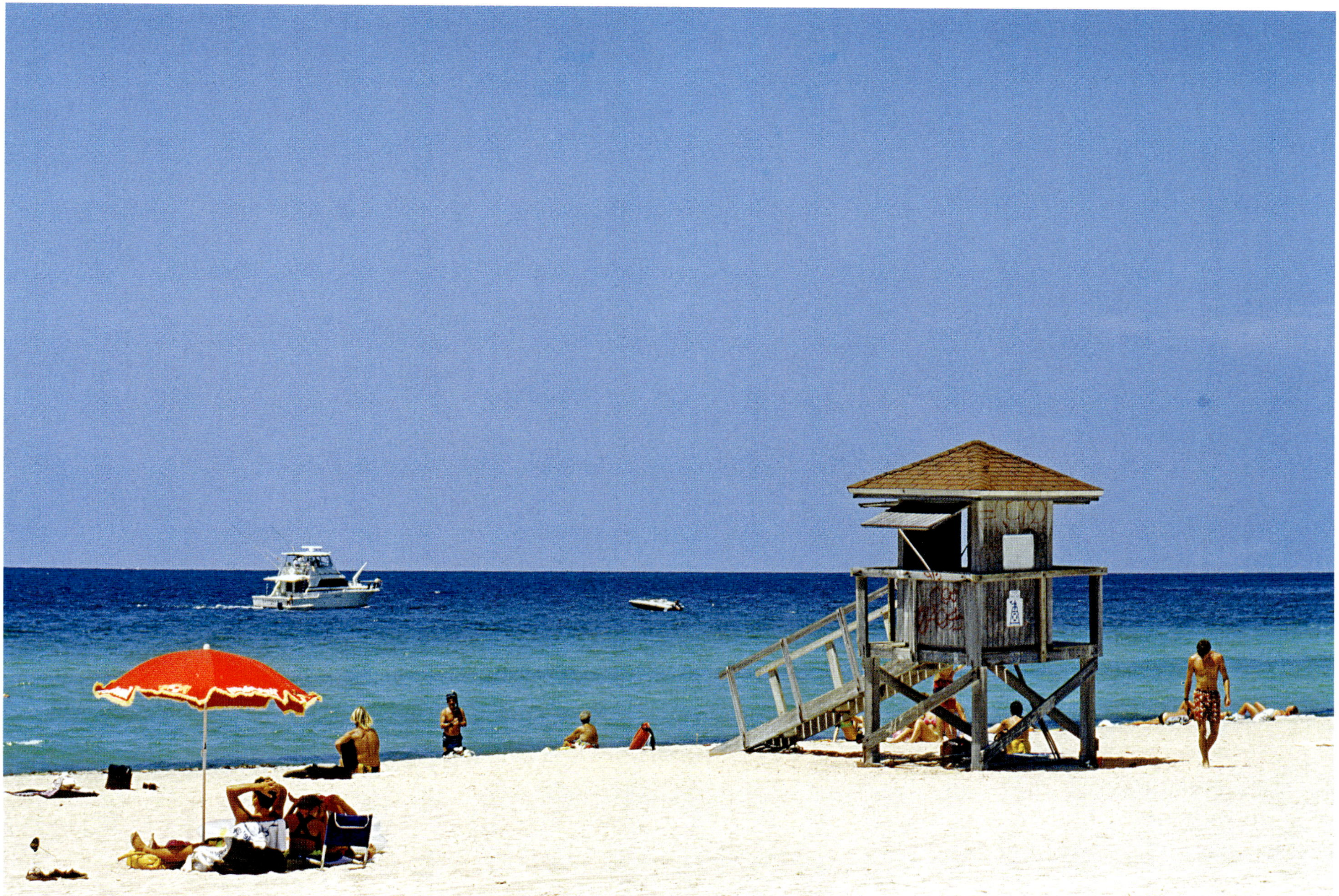